THE MORAL POLICE

THE MORAL POLICE

SURVIVING **DISCRIMINATION** IN **LAW ENFORCEMENT** AND **INJUSTICE** IN THE **COURTS**

JANELLE PEREZ

COPYRIGHT © 2020 JANELLE PEREZ
All rights reserved.

THE MORAL POLICE
*Surviving Discrimination in Law Enforcement
and Injustice in the Courts*

ISBN   978-1-5445-1759-9   *Hardcover*
         978-1-5445-1760-5   *Paperback*
         978-1-5445-1761-2   *Ebook*

To all women who have faced discrimination.

Also, to my children—to teach you to stand up for what is right.

CONTENTS

AUTHOR'S NOTE 9

INTRODUCTION 11

1. THE MARRIAGE AND THE AFFAIR 17

2. THE LETTER AND THE INVESTIGATION 37

3. FIGHTING THE ACCUSATIONS 75

4. THE COVER-UP 93

5. FILING THE LAWSUIT 123

6. GETTING MY STORY HEARD 155

7. THE APPEAL 177

8. THE DEATH OF A JUDGE 191

CONCLUSION 203

ACKNOWLEDGMENTS 211

ABOUT THE AUTHOR 213

AUTHOR'S NOTE

Throughout this book, names and identifying information have been changed for some individuals. Where dialogue appears, it is intended to recreate the essence of conversations rather than to be taken as verbatim quotes.

INTRODUCTION

Every single person is one bad decision away from a completely different life. I kept this belief in mind as I closed the door on a naked woman who was screaming incoherently in the back of my police cruiser. I'd answered a call about a disturbance at a cheap little hotel in a rundown part of the city, and when I arrived, I found this woman high out of her mind on drugs. I got her safely into my car, treating her with the same respect I'd shown to the man who had called several hours earlier to report a stolen car.

As I drove the woman to the station, I thought of my own family. I was familiar with what drug addiction could do to a person; I'd seen my aunts and uncles in the throes of addiction. I'd also seen them sober. I knew them to be good people who had their lives taken away by one bad decision.

Every decision has a consequence. I didn't judge the

woman who was high and raving in my back seat. In the course of my police work, I've seen so many people make the wrong decisions in their weakest moments. I wondered how her life would change as a result of the decisions she made that day.

One bad decision ended up changing my life, too. When I was a police officer, I was married and later separated from my husband. I started dating a fellow officer who had separated from his wife. Though our relationship wasn't against any police officer codes of conduct, it became the subject of an internal affairs investigation. I was fired. He was not.

Maybe I could have seen that coming; I'd been on the receiving end of gender discrimination in my police department previous to my termination. During the investigation into our relationship, it took all my energy to stay calm and ask questions about procedure and protocol. Even after the investigation concluded, my behavior was scrutinized. I was labeled as angry and argumentative for asking questions about department policy. Meanwhile, my male counterpart stormed into his superior's office and yelled at the lieutenant—but his outburst was brushed off as an understandable need to vent. Though I'd done nothing wrong, my superiors judged me for my marital status and treated me far more harshly than my counterpart. He raved at his boss and kept his job. I calmly asserted myself and lost my career.

I consulted with a lawyer who thought I had a strong case, and I filed a lawsuit against the city for wrongful termination, gender discrimination, violation of civil rights, and violation of due process. During the lawsuit, I felt invigorated: I wasn't going to roll over and move on with my life like my superiors probably expected me to. I was going to stand up for myself and take my power back with my voice.

My case initially lost at summary judgment, and I was crushed. It seemed crystal clear to me that I had been discriminated against—why was I the only person who could see the injustice that had been done? I wondered if there was something wrong with me. I felt fragile and uncertain. I nearly threw in the towel. But I'm not a quitter; I dug deep— rock-bottom deep—and found the tenacity to continue. I would not allow my voice to be taken away.

After years of legal battles, I won the violation of civil rights claim in the 9th Circuit Court of Appeals. When I got the news of this victory, I felt validated—I wasn't delusional or crazy; the discrimination I'd experienced really happened, and it wasn't right. I reveled in the judges' ruling that "any reasonable official would have been on notice that, viewing the facts in the light most favorable to her, Perez's termination was unconstitutional." I was going to get my day in court, to show the pattern of discrimination to a jury of my peers.

Then in a cruel twist of fate, one of the presiding judges

on my case died. The case was swiftly reheard (which is not standard practice with all court cases), one of the original judges changed his mind, and the initial decision was reversed. I lost.

If I could take back that one decision to begin that relationship, I would in a heartbeat. I believe in regrets. The relationship was not worth my job, the money I paid in attorney's fees, or the years I spent thinking about everything that went wrong as I tried to defend myself against decision-makers from the chief of police to the judges in the 9th Circuit Court of Appeals.

I'm telling my story here because I know I'm not the only one who has gone unheard by people in power. Ellen Pao, former interim CEO of Reddit, faced a similar scenario, which she wrote about in her memoir *Reset: My Fight for Inclusion and Lasting Change*. In the book, Pao describes how she had a brief relationship with a married coworker while she worked at Kleiner Perkins and suffered gender discrimination and retaliation. She filed a lawsuit against the firm for gender discrimination. She was later fired for "underperformance." While she lost the case, her suit inspired many other women in tech to speak up and file their own discrimination lawsuits against their employers.

I'm grateful for these women and others who stood up for themselves and paved the way for women with the same struggles to come forward. I'm grateful for women like Madeleine Albright—a female minority surrounded by powerful men in the halls of government—who I saw speak at a conference in 2019. She told the audience of mostly women that she refuses to be quiet. That every person's voice matters. Listening to her, I realized if I have the opportunity to expose the injustice I'd faced, it was my obligation to use my voice for the betterment of the world.

It took me seven years to find my voice. Along this multiyear-long journey, I discovered it's okay to not be okay. It's okay to be angry, sad, mad, passionate—any of the emotions in our natural range of experience. I turned to therapy, writing, exercising, spending time alone, speaking with confidantes, and listening to music to heal. I've learned that being brave and courageous is far from easy—but it is necessary.

When women decide to speak up, we're labeled as problematic and argumentative. Despite that label, I refuse to be shut out or swept under the rug. I feel empowered to count myself among a group of strong women who rightfully acknowledge what has happened in our workplaces and in our legal system, who are standing up to defend ourselves against the discrimination we've faced. I am one of many.

One decision tanked my career and changed my life. I hope my decision to speak up changes the lives of women who are finding their courage to give voice to the discrimination they've faced. When I was fighting the injustice done to me, I needed to hear stories like mine to know I was not alone. If you have experienced discrimination and bigotry in your workplace, in the legal system, or in your community, I hope my story helps you stand up and share yours. It takes a strong group of us to challenge policy and create change, and we inspire courage in each other when we share our stories.

What follows is the story of how I was wronged, how I fought, and how I continue to use my voice—for me, for you, and for every woman who was ever made to feel she was worth less than a man.

CHAPTER 1

THE MARRIAGE AND THE AFFAIR

The relationship that ended my career began innocuously enough. I'd been with the Roseville Police Department a few months when Bret Brzyscz, one of my field training officers, invited the team out together for drinks at a local bar one Friday after work. He enjoyed having the team meet up every so often, but they hadn't had one of these hangouts in a while. I'd just left field training, and I was on my own. It seemed like a good idea to meet up and build rapport with the guys at my new department.

We all walked into a little hole-in-the-wall bar not too far from the station, and around eight of us sat at a circular table. I don't remember what drink I ordered or who I sat next to, but I do remember I talked to Shad Begley. It was the first time I had a conversation with him outside of work.

We both have kids, and I asked how old his were and where they went to school. It was innocent small talk.

A couple of weeks later, we were all trying to find a time for the team to meet up again, but none of the times worked. Shad and I could both go, but no one else could make it. There was just one other person we hadn't invited: Asher Martin. I wasn't a fan of Asher at all, and I didn't want to ask him to come hang out with us.

The way I saw it, Asher was the chief's protégé. The chief had been a captain at the Sacramento Police Department, and when he transferred to Roseville, he took several of his guys with him. Asher Martin was one of them. When police officers transfer from one department to another, they have to go through a probationary period at their new department. When an officer is on probation, they can be terminated at any time, and the department does not have to give cause.

I was shocked by how I perceived Asher to behave while he was on probation. I didn't agree with Asher's style of police work. I didn't like the way he talked to people while he was on calls; I thought he was disrespectful and rude. Frankly, it wasn't that different from his behavior in the office.

For example: during one meeting, the whole team was sitting in a briefing at the start of our shift. Asher was sitting next to a buddy of his, Blake Drew, who had also transferred from Sacramento. I was sitting across the table from them. As the sergeant delivered the briefing, Asher started to make this gesture with his mouth and hand—it looked to me like he was mimicking masturbation.

I thought it was incredibly inappropriate. I wondered why he would think that gesture was okay; Asher was new at the department, and he was on probation, just like me. I couldn't tell if the sergeant saw the gesture or not, but I wasn't going to be the one to speak up. I didn't want to be marked as a complainer. Blake didn't stop him, and nobody said anything.

Asher was not someone I wanted to talk to outside of work. As we started to set up the next team meetup, no one asked whether Asher was available. A bunch of people couldn't go, and I told Shad that if he wanted to invite Asher, that was on him, but I wasn't going to do it. Shad didn't invite him either. The next night, it was just Shad and me getting drinks at the bar.

I wanted to try someplace more modern, less of a dive, so we went to The Lounge. It was close to work and had a jukebox with decent music. I'd never been there before, but this meetup with Shad would turn into the first of many. The Lounge became our place. We stayed at The Lounge for hours, talking about our work, and then our families, and eventually our marriages.

The more we talked, the more I realized how much I enjoyed my time with Shad. He was relatable, and that was comforting. He wasn't happy, and neither was I. I felt like I could trust him. He told me stories from his deployment that he'd never told anyone, stories that haunted him. I was at a point in my life where I felt broken, and the more he talked about his military experience and the struggles with his marriage, I could tell Shad was really broken, too.

After a few hours, Shad said he needed to get going because his wife would wonder where he was.

I was at work a few days later, meeting with Asher, when a text came in from Shad on my work phone. *Miss me yet?* The truth was, I hadn't stopped thinking about him since we'd met for drinks. I knew better than to text him back on my work phone, so I texted back my personal cell phone number.

We continued to meet up at The Lounge after that, and as I opened up about my own unhappiness, our connection deepened. I told Shad about leaving my old police department to stay at home with my kids and how depressed I got before I finally decided to go back to work. We got vulnerable with each other quickly.

We'd only met up two or three times when I got a call from Shad at home one day. He said he wanted to separate from his wife and move out. I was shocked; it seemed like this major change in Shad's life was happening so fast. I realized how unhappy he must have been. At the same time, I took comfort in how much Shad shared with me. It seemed he trusted me. I liked that we confided in each other. When I talked to him, I felt like I was finally coming out of a miserable fog I'd been in for several years.

I think I was drawn to Shad because my connection with him was an echo of a past relationship with a man I'd loved and lost long before I got married, had kids, and changed police departments. I wanted Shad to be like Noah.

UNRESOLVED LOVE

Noah was married when I met him, and he later separated from his wife. He was my first field training officer when I started at the South San Francisco Police Department, though nothing happened between us until much later. We got to know each other well while we worked together, and after eighteen months, I got off probation. Noah and I talked often, as friends only. When I told him I was thinking about going on a date with someone, Noah told me not to. He said the man wasn't good for me. I started to wonder if Noah said that because he wanted to date me. I remember going out with a girlfriend one night, and we met up with Noah and one of his friends. As we sipped drinks together, Noah massaged my leg under the table. At that point, I knew we were both interested in each other. We started dating, and we were together for almost a year.

Noah's dad had died when he was a teenager, and his aunt looked after him financially after that. When Noah wanted to buy a house in the Bay Area, his aunt gave him money for the down payment. She constantly paid for extravagances and vacations. Once, when Noah was housesitting for his aunt, I went over to her house and made him dinner. When she got back into town, I decided to go over to her house and introduce myself. When I told her I was Noah's girlfriend, she told me frankly that she didn't support our relationship. It seemed to me that she owned him. And she thought Noah should be with his ex.

She arranged a vacation to Disney World for Noah, his son, and his ex. I wasn't comfortable with him going on family trips with his ex. I told Noah that if he decided to go on the trip, we'd be done.

Noah and I were still in conflict when I got a call from his mom out of the blue. I'd never met her. But she called to plead with me. "Noah loves you," she said, "and he doesn't want to lose you by going on this trip. If he does go, and his ex goes, can you think about staying with him?"

My jaw was on the floor. I couldn't believe Noah's mom would call me to try to save his relationship with me. The next morning, Noah called and said he was going on the trip. Then he hung up on me. I dropped to the floor and sobbed like I never had before. My dad was there, and he picked me up off the floor and held me. Our family wasn't particularly affectionate; we didn't hug much when I was growing up. But that day, my dad comforted me while I cried.

The day Noah came back from the trip, I happened to be at a party at my friend's house down the street from where he lived. I hadn't heard from him, so I went by his house. The door was wide open, so I walked in—I stayed there a lot, and it wasn't unusual for me to just pop in—and there was Noah's ex.

"Oh," she said, "you must be Janelle."

"I am," I said, and then I realized my car was blocking the driveway. I'd only stopped by to see if Noah was home. I turned around to go move my car. Noah's voice rang out behind me: "Janelle, don't leave."

His ex left, and I stayed to talk. "I think it's better if we're not together right now," Noah said. "But I think you're my soulmate, and we're supposed to be together. I think we'll be together again one day. I just don't know when."

I felt the same way for him. I thought Noah was my soulmate, and I was his, but the trip had torn us apart. Hearing him say we were supposed to be together gave me hope that maybe someday we could be. At the same time, that hope didn't feel fair. I went into a downward spiral after that, dating guys here and there to try to take the pain away. All the while, I was tormented by the idea that he'd left the door open, and it could be possible to get back together.

Noah got a special assignment, and he always worked off-site, so I didn't see him much after that. I heard he got back together with his ex, and I could feel the stares from other officers' wives who knew her and knew our history.

I worked in South San Francisco for several more years, and in that time, experienced multiple toxic relationships with men who didn't value me. Then I met Jason. He was the most selfless and kind man I'd ever met, and I believed in my heart he would never hurt me. I knew I wanted to have a family, and I knew Jason would be a good dad. We got married and had a son.

BUILDING A FAMILY

My decision to marry Jason was mostly functional; I didn't have faith in marriage, and I didn't see marriage as final. My memories of my parents' marriage were painful, filled with constant fighting. I remember huddling in the bedroom I shared with my sister. We each hid in our beds as we listened to our parents scream and yell at each other.

They slammed doors. We could hear them breaking things. Looking back, I can see now how toxic that was for us as young children, but it was the example I grew up with. As an adult, I held no sanctity in marriage.

When I was pregnant with my second child, I decided to quit the department to stay at home with my children. Jason and I knew the only way we could afford to live off of one income was to live outside of the San Francisco Bay Area. We found a house a few hours away in Lincoln. After we bought it, we kept our place in South San Francisco for a little while longer while I worked, and we spent weekends in our new home. I planned to stop working at some point, but I wasn't quite ready yet.

Then, one day when I was eight weeks pregnant with my second child, there was an accident with my son. My mom agreed to watch him while I went to work, so I took him over to her house. My sister and her husband were there, and before I left, we were all in the backyard, where my mom had a basketball hoop on a concrete pad. My sister's husband put my son up on his shoulders and walked forward for them to shoot a basket. He took his hands off my son's legs for just a moment, and my son toppled backward and fell headfirst onto the concrete.

He wasn't moving. I remember picking him up, and I remember my sister calling 911. I rode with my son in the ambulance and called Jason to have him leave work and meet us at the hospital. I cried the whole way.

At the hospital, as my son was being sent through a CT machine, I worried about the baby just beginning to grow in my belly. The hospital techs wouldn't let me be with my son because I was pregnant and needed to keep my distance from the imaging machines. I worried I would lose my son lying on the table, and I worried I would lose the child in my belly. It was the worst day of my life.

I called my sergeant and told him I needed to give my two weeks' notice and burn all my vacation time immediately. I didn't trust anyone to care for my son, not even Jason. I needed to protect him while his skull healed.

When my second child was born, I suffered from postpartum depression. Depression was hard for me to recognize, much less admit to, because I'd trained myself in law enforcement to be the strong one who was there for other people. I responded to calls for help, and it was much, much harder for me to call for help myself.

Within a month of the birth of our second child, it was clear I needed a stronger support system. I felt overwhelmed by the responsibilities of caring for a toddler and an infant, even with Jason on leave to help. We decided to move two hours away to be closer to my mom and sister. I wanted to be near family.

I thought I would be happier when I had more support, but I wasn't. I was still miserable, and I couldn't figure out the cause.

Then one night, I was thinking about Noah, and I got emotional. Jason asked me what was wrong, and I told him the truth: before I met him, I had been in love with Noah, and I truly thought he was the one I would spend my life with. When Noah ended things, he said it wasn't our time, but we would be together again. I realized I never had closure in my relationship with him. That night, while I cried and described the relationship to Jason, I realized that without closure to move on from my relationship with Noah, I couldn't move forward in my marriage with Jason. My marriage was unhappy because I was unhappy. Jason hadn't known how much I needed to work on myself in order to be in a healthy relationship. He didn't get angry or upset. He just listened and told me to do whatever I needed to do to help myself heal.

Perhaps that's the moment I should have separated from Jason. I needed time to reflect on my past and figure out the next step forward. And yet, as a mother of two young kids, I had to keep going with our chaotic, day-to-day lives. There wasn't time to feel the pain of that unresolved relationship, much less come up with a strategy for overcoming it.

Twenty-four hours a day, seven days a week, there was no break from the insanity of caring for two young children. I didn't have any time to process all my feelings and emotions. I love my children more than anything else in the world, and I felt so confused. I remember one day when I took my kids for a long walk to the park, and the whole time I was thinking about how unfair my life was. Why did I have to give up my job to stay at home with the kids and my husband got to keep his? How, when I have two such precious gifts, could I be so unhappy?

For my own mental health, I needed to have something that was just for me. I wanted to find anything that would help me feel like my "old self." Eventually, I thought that what must be missing was work. My job had given me a sense of purpose, and I remembered feeling happier when I was working.

RETURN TO WORK

I got a job with the Roseville Police Department, which was a fifteen-minute drive from our old home in Lincoln. We moved back. I'd taken a short enough break from service that I'd been hired as a lateral police officer, meaning I would have a shorter field training program. New hires out of the academy typically have to do six months of field training; I would only be required to do eight weeks.

Though as I would soon see after joining the department, not all lateral hires were treated equally. Asher Martin, for example, only did six weeks of field training. Blake Drew had less experience as a police officer, and only did seven weeks. Blake started at Roseville on the same day I did, and when he was released from training and allowed to go out on his own, I asked one of my field training officers if I could be done early, too. I'd done well in field training, and all my supervisors had given me positive feedback. Still, my field training officer said no to my request. It was hard to swallow, watching my male counterparts being cut loose much sooner than I was.

Later, after I'd been terminated, I asked Shad to look through the calendar system where the start dates and exit dates for each officer's field training were recorded. A sergeant was in charge of scheduling, but it wasn't clear who made the decision to end an officer's field training early. I never knew why I had to put in more time than other officers who'd been lateral hires. It clearly had nothing to do with differences in performance. I suspected it was because I was a woman. In fact, I was one of only around six women in a department of approximately 127 officers.

A little while into my field training, I was talking with a

sergeant, Missy Morris, who recommended a book to me called *Emotional Survival for Law Enforcement*. She told me to read the book and report back to her to set up a time to talk about it. I didn't report to Morris, but that didn't matter; when a superior tells you to do something, you do it. I did what I was told, and I started to read the book.

Shortly after speaking with Morris, I was in the car with my field training officer, Bret. "What are you doing after work?" he asked.

"I have to go home and read a book Morris assigned to me," I told him.

"What are you talking about?"

"She told me to read *Emotional Survival for Law Enforcement*," I said, "and then I have to meet with her after."

"On your own time?" he asked.

"Well, yeah," I replied.

I was driving at the time, and he immediately asked me to pull over. He'd never heard of a probationary officer being told to read a book, he said. He didn't know of any of the other probationary officers reading the book.

"If you're being asked to do something as part of your job, you should be paid for it," he said.

He got out of the car and called Morris. "What's the story with this book?" he asked. He felt that as a field training officer, he needed to know what the expectations were for the new people he worked with.

Morris admitted that she'd told me to read the book. She said she was asking all the new officers to read it. If Bret didn't like it, well, that was just too bad.

Bret didn't stop there. He called Lieutenant Maria Richardson, who was the supervisor in charge. He told her he didn't think it was fair that I was the only one being asked to read this book and that I had to do it on my own time. Richardson said she'd look into it.

About five minutes later, Richardson called Bret back. I didn't hear the conversation, but apparently, she told him that I didn't have to read the book. I don't remember him actually telling me at the time to stop reading the book, but if he had, I would have continued reading it anyway. Bret was just an officer, like me, and since I'd been ordered by a supervisor to read the book, I decided I'd continue reading it until one of the supervisors told me to stop. None of them ever did.

I think Bret saw that I was a competent, experienced officer, and he didn't appreciate these supervisors throwing their weight around and taking advantage of a trainee by forcing me to do something during my off-duty hours.

After the car ride with Bret, I asked Blake Drew if he'd been told to read the book, and he said no, but he'd read it before.

After I finished the book, I dropped it back off in Morris's office, and then I ran into her in the bathroom. I told her I was done with the book and asked when she wanted to meet to talk about it. She offered to talk about it right then and there, so we had a five-minute conversation in the bathroom, and we went our separate ways.

I asked around to other officers about the book, and it turned out no one else had been required to read it. I didn't make an issue of it because I was still on probation. I knew it wasn't the time to ask questions or raise concerns. I didn't want to be seen as a problem or to give the department any reason to let me go.

On a training day, I ran into Morris again at the outdoor shooting range. I was walking to the porta-potties when she caught up with me. Out of the blue, she asked, "Why would you ever leave your kids at home and come back to a job if you didn't have to?"

I was stunned. And offended. Morris didn't know me; she knew nothing of my family or my home life. I thought her question was incredibly rude. But I was still on probation, so I laughed off her question and kept walking.

During depositions, my lawyer asked Morris if she recalled asking why I chose to work rather than stay at home with my children. "I don't specifically remember that, no," Morris responded. While the question may not have been memorable for her, it certainly was for me.

THE SEPARATION

By the time I'd left field training and Bret asked the whole team to go out for drinks, I was still feeling overwhelmed and broken. I was still struggling in my marriage, still trying to keep up with a demanding home life with two young kids, and walking on eggshells at work until I was through probation. When I talked to Shad, I felt relief in recognizing a fellow damaged person, and we took comfort in confiding in each other.

We were both going through difficult times, and we lent each other support. I didn't feel an instant connection to Shad, but I think he reminded me a little of Noah. I wanted him to be Noah. I still felt so unresolved about my relationship with Noah that it was affecting my marriage to Jason. I knew that I needed time to let myself move on from

Noah, but until I met Shad, I didn't have the strength to leave my marriage.

I was shocked when, in April, Shad told me he was separating from his wife. His decision helped me with my own resolve: a week or so later, I decided to separate from Jason.

The first person I told about my separation and my attraction to Shad was my dad. "Don't get involved with Shad," he said. "You need to get off probation first. I know how supervisors work. They can make up any reason to fire you. Wait to see Shad until you're done with probation."

There were no rules against two officers dating, so there was nothing wrong with Shad and I starting a relationship. Just like there would have been nothing "wrong" with me asking questions about why I had to stay longer in field training than anyone else, or why I had to read a book no one else was required to read, or why Asher Martin could make what I perceived as inappropriate gestures in a meeting in front of the sergeant with no repercussions.

But my dad knew, just as I did, that it was important not to call attention to myself during probation. I didn't want to be labeled as difficult, combative, or unsupportive. But I also didn't want my work to dictate my relationships. I didn't think it was possible—or fair—for them to terminate me based on whom I decided to become involved with. In fact,

I'd heard rumors from multiple people that some of the male officers in the department were involved in swingers' clubs, but I hadn't heard of anyone receiving reprimand or punishment for it. I also knew men on the SWAT team who disregarded the city's ban on using tobacco products. Blatantly. They chewed tobacco in front of Captain Stefan Moore, the head of the SWAT team, and to my knowledge, no one was ever reprimanded or investigated. How threatening could my off-duty relationship be?

If I'd taken my dad's advice, it might have saved my career. Unfortunately, I didn't. But before I understood the consequences, and after we'd each separated from our spouses, Shad and I decided to date.

I also started going to therapy. It was incredibly helpful to have a neutral space to talk about my marriage and my kids, to dig deeper into the unresolved issues of my past and how they affected me in the present, and to gain confidence and knowledge for dealing with present-day issues in healthy ways. I was ready to confront my issues head-on, slay some of my demons, and come to terms with my regrets.

I didn't know then that my relationship with Shad would become my biggest regret.

CHAPTER 2

THE LETTER AND THE INVESTIGATION

Jason and I had separated, but for a short time, we still lived in the same house. He slept in a room downstairs. One day when Jason was out of town, Shad and I were off duty and hanging out at my house.

Then my phone buzzed. The text was from Jason. "Who's at the house right now, and what are you doing?"

My stomach clenched into a hard knot. I glanced over at Shad, who was lounging on the couch. I hadn't yet told Jason I was dating anyone. I typed back, "What are you talking about?"

"The neighbor saw a car pull into the garage, and then the garage door shut. He said the car hasn't left."

Panic flooded my mind. *I have to tell him now,* I thought. I did not feel ready to have that conversation. In the next moment, the panic mixed with anger. *How could the neighbors be so nosy? They're not friends.* I was pissed. They didn't know Jason and I had separated, and they had no context for why someone else's car might be in the garage. I felt violated. *Why would they spy on me like that and then text Jason without talking to me first?*

I told Shad about the text messages. "I think you should go," I said. "Clearly, the neighbors are waiting for your car to leave."

Shad agreed and picked up his keys. As he backed out of the garage, I wondered if the neighbors were watching.

Jason got home later the next day, and neither of us talked about our text exchange. The kids were in bed, and I wasn't going to start what I knew would be an intense conversation in the middle of the night.

But Jason was hell-bent on finding out who had come over to the house. I didn't want to tell him about my relationship; I wasn't sure what he was going to do. Jason looked at the phone records and found calls from a number he didn't recognize—the landline Shad had been calling me from. Shad was living at another officer's house while he was separated from his wife, and he'd been calling me on the house phone.

So when Jason searched the phone records, it wasn't Shad's name that came up; it was the other officer with whom he'd been staying. Jason at first assumed it was this other officer I'd been seeing, but it didn't take him long to figure out the final pieces of the puzzle.

When Jason found out it was Shad's car in the garage that night, he played it cool. He seemed like he was going to try and be understanding of the situation. Instead of telling me his next move, he called Shad's wife, Eleanor Mann.

I didn't know any of this was happening until one day when I was sitting in my police car, and a call came in from Shad. All the details came out at once: Jason and Eleanor had not only talked, but they'd met up in person, and Jason had told her everything he had found out about our relationship.

Jason later told me what he said to Eleanor: that he suspected Shad had been visiting me at home because the neighbor had seen Shad's car pull into the garage. Jason also told Eleanor that I sometimes met Shad at Louie Young's house, where he had been staying after his separation. After hearing this, Eleanor emailed Shad and threatened to send a letter to the Roseville Police Department to get him fired.

Shad told me he'd sent a response back to reason with her. She didn't work, and Shad's job was their family's sole source of income. It would be irresponsible, he argued, to jeopardize his livelihood, as it provided for her and the kids.

As Shad told me all of this, my mind raced. I tried to think through everything we needed to do to keep things from getting worse. I told Shad to make sure he had a strong password on his email so she couldn't get into it. I told him I wouldn't text him from then on in case she was monitoring our communication. I told him to get a separate phone account that she didn't know about.

At work, we had computers in each of the cars that we could use to message fellow officers, but I'd already known better than to use those to send personal messages while on the job. I hadn't sent him any emails through our work accounts. I knew not to use my work phone for personal communication. At the time, I thought I'd been smart in all these precautions. I thought it was enough to protect me and my job.

Even though I knew I hadn't broken any of the rules, I still thought back to the warning my dad had given me: "Don't date Shad while you're on probation. They could use any reason at all to fire you."

I hung up the call with Shad. As I dialed Jason's number,

my worry gave way to rage. When he picked up, I went off on him. "What were you thinking?" I yelled. "Don't you realize you're messing with someone's job? With *my* job?"

When Jason and I talk about this now, years later, he regrets having told Eleanor Mann. He didn't realize then what an explosive effect that one conversation would have on our lives. He couldn't have known then that I would ultimately lose my job, just as my dad had warned.

THE LETTER

A few weeks later, in early June of 2012, Eleanor Mann sent a letter to Daniel Hahn, the chief of police in Roseville, claiming that Shad and I were sneaking around and conducting an affair while on duty. In her letter, which was discussed in the court records, Eleanor claimed that Shad's interactions with me had to be taking place while we were in uniform because Shad "always came home on time after work and spent his off days with our three young daughters and me."

Shad's free time "was spent at home," she insisted, so his affair with me had to have occurred on duty when Shad and I worked the same shift. "The relationship would have to have developed while he was on duty as a police officer and most likely with someone who was on duty with him," Eleanor told Hahn. Eleanor went on to say that she had obtained copies of Shad's telephone and text logs and determined that there were numerous phone calls and texts between Shad and me.

While Eleanor made it sound like Shad was frequently at home when he wasn't working, the truth was that Shad had moved out around four weeks before. He wanted a divorce. Eleanor mentioned this in her letter to Hahn, but indicated that Shad's "sudden and shocking" news didn't make sense until she got Jason's call.

THE INTERNAL AFFAIRS INVESTIGATION BEGINS

Eleanor hadn't told Shad she was sending the letter. He found out the next day when he went into work and was pulled into Lieutenant Troy Bergstrom's office. Bergstrom told Shad that the city had received the letter and that he was now the subject of an internal affairs (IA) investigation into Eleanor Mann's allegations.

When Shad's break came, he called me to give me a heads-up that I was going to be investigated, too. I was at home, off duty. My relationship with Shad had, by that point, become a roller coaster with the highest of highs and the lowest of lows, and I couldn't say where on the track we were that day. But as soon as he told me about the investigation, I became incredibly angry.

I wanted to scream. *He should have known his ex would fuck with his career. Why hadn't he done more to protect himself, to protect me?*

I understood what it felt like to be as angry as she must have been to have sent that letter. But I would never have done something like that. She had displayed her jealousy and anger as publicly as possible. I would never have messed with two people's careers over my own pain. I kept trying to reassure myself: *we didn't do anything illegal or against policy.*

As I got ready to go to work that evening, I was nervous. I didn't know the content of the letter at that point or what Eleanor had alleged, and I had no idea what questions Bergstrom would ask.

A few months before, I'd been pulled in as a witness for an IA investigation for Asher Martin. I'd been nervous then, too, because I didn't know what questions the investigators would ask me. I believe Asher had been accused of being rude and unprofessional on a traffic stop I'd witnessed. Asher had raised his voice, and he appeared to me to have been obnoxious; that was the way Asher was with everyone on the street. But he hadn't done anything criminal, and there was no way I was going to go into the investigation and say, "Asher was a total dick." I knew to only give short, direct answers to the investigator's questions.

As I stepped into Bergstrom's office, I saw he wasn't alone. Standing with Bergstrom was Morris, the sergeant who'd told me to read the book and who had asked me how I could leave my kids at home and come back to work. I thought, *What the hell is she doing here?* I didn't know her, and I certainly hadn't asked her to be there. But I said nothing.

Much later, during the depositions for the case I brought against the city of Roseville, Bergstrom described to my lawyer why he decided to bring Morris into the room:

> Lawyer: Was there a reason why you decided to include Sergeant Morris?
>
> Bergstrom: This internal affairs investigation was a little different. You know, it's not your use of force and being rude to somebody in the field kind of IA. The type of allegation that it was, I thought it might make Officer Perez feel more comfortable if Sergeant Morris was there when I gave her the letter because Sergeant Morris is also female [...]
>
> Lawyer: How did you notify Shad about the internal investigation?
>
> Bergstrom: Same way.
>
> Lawyer: Was Sergeant Morris with you when you notified Shad?

Bergstrom: No.

Lawyer: What was the reason why you didn't include Sergeant Morris with you when you notified Shad?

Bergstrom: Because Shad is male. And again, the whole reason I had Sergeant Morris sit in when I notified Officer Perez is because Sergeant Morris is female and Officer Perez is female. Considering we were about to give her a notice that was about inappropriate sexual activity, I thought it would make her feel more comfortable. I also didn't know—we had a few conversations, but I know Officer Begley, so it's different.

Bergstrom's assumption that just having another woman in the room would make me feel more comfortable couldn't have been further from the truth. I didn't care for Morris, and I certainly didn't feel any more comfortable knowing that she was there to hear about the allegations being made about me.

What made me the most upset was that Bergstrom had treated me differently than he treated Shad, a man. I later asked Shad if Bergstrom had anyone else in the office with him when he told Shad about the allegations, and Shad said no. The tacit assumption seemed to be that Shad was tough and strong and didn't need anyone to support him, but I might be emotional and weak, so it would be best to have another female in the room. The respect I'd had for Bergstrom before that point flew out the window.

I had to do all the same tests as the men to get hired. I had to jump a six-foot wall, drag a weighted dummy, and run timed drills. I didn't get it any easier because I was a woman—so I couldn't understand why Bergstrom would attempt to make it "easier" on me in a meeting that I would have preferred to stay private. I didn't need the support of another woman, and I certainly didn't get support from Morris.

Bergstrom handed me the letter explaining the IA investigation and my rights. The meeting was quick and simple. Bergstrom told me the department had received a citizen's complaint (Eleanor Mann's letter) and that an investigation would be made into the alleged on-duty relationship between Shad and me. The letter included an appointment time set for the following week for me to return for my interview. That was it.

THE INVESTIGATION INTERVIEWS

A few days later, Bergstrom interviewed Eleanor in a conference room at the Civic Center. Although Shad had moved out, Eleanor insisted that Shad and I had "developed" our relationship while on duty because Shad "always came home on time after work." Then her story started to unravel. She admitted that on the night Jason had called her,

Shad had been driving his personal vehicle and was not on duty. Eleanor also revealed that she didn't have any firsthand knowledge that I was meeting Shad at Louie Young's house while I was on duty.

Eleanor's accusations about phone calls and texting also proved sketchy. Per Bergstrom's report, "She was not able to obtain a log of when these texts were sent or who they were sent to because she was not the account holder." Although Shad's text messaging jumped, Eleanor admitted she had no idea who was receiving the texts or when they were sent. "She assumed that to send that many texts that Shad must have been texting Officer Perez while on duty," Bergstrom wrote in his report.

Bergstrom talked with Jason a few hours later. He immediately asked Jason about finding Shad and me at my house in Lincoln. Jason said everything Shad and I had done occurred while we were off duty.

Jason told Bergstrom that he and I were mending our relationship through therapy and that he had "actually become friends with Officer Begley." Eleanor, on the other hand, was "one angry lady," Jason told Bergstrom. He and Eleanor had talked a few times over the phone, Jason said, but he'd stopped talking with her because of how angry she was.

Later, when Bergstrom interviewed Louie, who let Shad

stay at his house after he split from Eleanor, Louie said he'd never seen Shad and me together at his house in uniform or on duty. Louie noted that his son lives with him and that Shad "would never do anything inappropriate."

Things were not shaping up to be as clear-cut as Eleanor's original letter suggested. If Shad and I were having an illicit affair, why is it that my estranged husband was becoming friends with Shad? If we were running around having sexual liaisons while in uniform, how is it that none of the prying neighbors or roommates ever saw us in uniform driving police cruisers?

From Bergstrom's report:

> "I specifically asked Eleanor if she had any knowledge of or if Shad had told her about any sexual contact between the two officers while they were on duty, and she had no information regarding that occurring nor had Shad said anything like that to her."

Still, Bergstrom kept at it. He analyzed the phone records Eleanor provided. If he was expecting an avalanche of text messages and phone calls between Shad and me while we were on duty, he was sorely disappointed.

Focusing on nine days from May 12 to May 21, only five of which I worked, Bergstrom found that we'd exchanged fifteen calls on our private phones during that time. Nine had been initiated by Shad. The longest call during that time occurred on one of my vacation days. A few others occurred while I was en route to a service call or returning from a call. I had one call while on a lunch break. A few of the really short one-, two-, or three-minute calls could have been voicemail messages; Bergstrom didn't know because he didn't bother to check. They also checked our work phones but didn't find anything.

Another thing that bothered me was how Eleanor had gotten these phone records. Shad was separated from Eleanor, and he was the account holder of his personal phone account. Shad never gave them to her and never gave her permission to access them, which he told my lawyer during his deposition.

> Lawyer: [Eleanor] got access to those records after your date of separation in April of 2012, right? [...] If you know.
>
> Begley: It's my understanding it was after, yes.
>
> Lawyer: Did you ever give her authorization to obtain those records?
>
> Begley: No.
>
> Lawyer: If you know, you may not, did you know specifi-

cally how she went about obtaining those records without your authorization?

Begley: There were two ways I know she could have: Either online or if she opened the mail. I moved out of the house, so my phone records, the bill, I think, was still going there. But I think she got online. I think she went online, logged in to the account, and printed them.

In fact, Shad told me that he filed a police report about Eleanor obtaining his phone records without his permission. In his rebuttal letter to Chief Hahn on August 30, 2012, which later became part of the court record, Shad said the cell phone records had been "illegally obtained."

> I consulted with a divorce attorney and am well aware that from the point of separation [from Eleanor Mann on April 25, 2012], my cell phone and my cell phone bill was my personal property, and she did not legally have the right to be in possession of it. Had I been asked [during the IA investigation], I could have explained that her name was nowhere on that phone account, and she never had permission to be in possession of it. In fact, the only way she became in possession of my cell phone bill was to have created an account, pretending to be me, and then printing out paperwork that she illegally obtained. She sent the cell phone bill to the Roseville Police Department, and the bill was reviewed, searched, and an investigation was conducted, and never

once did I give my permission to have my personal cell phone bill searched.

However, Bergstrom and his superiors didn't seem to care that the records they used in their investigation were obtained illegally. If anyone should be sensitive to that, it should be a cop. No court in the country would allow the police to use illegally obtained documents to prosecute a case against someone. In my case, the IA investigation was *based* on fraudulently acquired records, according to Shad, and never should have been allowed to proceed.

Bergstrom met with Shad and Shad's representative from the police officers' union, Sam Snow, at one o'clock in the afternoon on June 15. The meeting lasted less than twenty minutes. Bergstrom told Shad about Eleanor's complaint and explained that Shad was being investigated to determine whether he had behaved in a manner that was unbecoming an officer or had engaged in conduct that interfered with his police work.

Shad was forthcoming. Yes, he was in a relationship with Officer Perez. No, they had never had any inappropriate contact on duty. He had never met her at his home while on duty. No, he didn't meet her for lunch or breaks any more than he met with other members of his team. The relationship had never compromised his work as a police officer. Toward the end of the conversation, Snow asked Bergstrom to please look at Shad's work performance. That will tell you if his performance was unsatisfactory, Snow said.

Then, Shad said, in his deposition, Bergstrom seemed to try to put Shad at ease.

>Lawyer: Did Bergstrom do your IA interview?
>
>Begley: Yes.
>
>Lawyer: You wrote also, "turned off recorder in my interview." Did Lieutenant Bergstrom turn off the recorder?
>
>Begley: Yes.
>
>Lawyer: Did he tell you that "this was not a big deal" during that IA interview?
>
>Begley: Yes.

In Bergstrom's deposition, the lieutenant denied having said this but seemed to describe the events about the same way.

>Lawyer: Did you tell Shad Begley that you thought the investigation was not a big deal?
>
>Bergstrom: No. What—at the end of all my internal affairs

investigations, I kind of have the same spiel [...] usually we are done with the interview. We're done—we're past the formal part of the interview, the tape recorder is off. We're just wrapping a few things up, and I will explain to people basically what's left in the process. Give them kind of a time frame, if I can give them a time frame. And in almost every one of those, I'll explain to them, Hey, look, don't make this bigger than what it is. Don't—because people will—they will stress out. You know, some things people have a right to stress out about, but other things, it's something small, and they go crazy [...] I learned that through internal affairs, if you can kind of calm them down from the beginning and not have them go off the deep end over things. And so I don't remember the specific wording of the conversation I had with Shad, but I have had the same conversations with just about every single person that I have had those interviews with.

I didn't know Bergstrom well, but Shad did. They were on the SWAT team together. They'd been to team barbecues, and both played in a golf tournament in honor of a fellow officer who had died. I knew they were close. When Bergstrom told Shad the investigation was no big deal, I trusted he meant it. I imagined the scenario from Bergstrom's perspective: Shad's crazy ex-wife had sent a letter, and the department's hands were tied. There was no other option but to investigate. Everything would be okay.

Clearly, by the end of it all, everything was not okay. Not in the least.

I met with Bergstrom about an hour later. In the week between Bergstrom notifying me of the IA investigation and my interview with him, I'd met with Phillip Craig, a representative from the police officers' union, to discuss my rights during the investigation. I told Craig everything that had happened from my perspective and asked him to sit in with me during the interview.

When I sat down in Bergstrom's office for my interview, I was on edge. Craig came into the office with me, and Bergstrom switched on a tape recorder. Bergstrom assured me the investigation was intended to determine what happened on duty. But his questions confused me. He asked whether I was involved in a relationship with Shad, and I told him yes, we were dating. I thought, *If you're only investigating on-duty behavior, why are you asking about my off-duty relationship?*

I didn't ask any questions, though. Being the subject of an IA investigation while on probation was already a big enough predicament. I was afraid to ask any question that might make my situation even more tenuous.

Bergstrom asked simplistic questions about how I used my cell phone at work. "When you use your work cell phone, is the call work-related?" he asked. I told him yes. "If you use your personal cell phone, is it a personal call?" I told him yes. It was common practice for officers to carry both their work phones and their personal phones with them while on duty, and officers regularly make short calls on their personal cell phones while on breaks or during downtime on shifts.

Bergstrom never asked if our calls took place while we were on lunch breaks, or foot patrol, or at Starbucks getting coffee. He never asked whether a particular entry in the log was an actual call or if it went to voicemail because one of us didn't answer while we were on duty.

Later, in Bergstrom's deposition during the court case, my lawyer asked Bergstrom about this line of questioning:

> Lawyer: Do you recall if any investigation was made into whether these phone calls were made during a code seven [the code for a lunch break during a shift] between Officer Begley and Officer Perez?
>
> Bergstrom: I didn't ask that, no.
>
> Lawyer: Would it have made a difference in your analysis?
>
> Bergstrom: It could.

But Bergstrom didn't gather information on our phone calls.

At the end of the interview, Bergstrom switched off the recorder. He still seemed relaxed. "We just have to do these interviews," he said. "It's not a big deal." The union representative stayed quiet. I felt stressed. In the back of my mind, my dad's voice kept repeating on loop: "They can fire you for no reason."

Throughout his investigation, Bergstrom reassured people that he wasn't interested in our private lives. He was only interested in our on-duty performance.

"My concern is work-related stuff," Bergstrom told Louie. "The complaint is that they were conducting a personal relationship, which off duty they can do whatever they want, but that it's impacting the work environment because they're conducting that relationship while on duty."

Bergstrom told Jason the same thing: "The complaint centers around what they are taking part in while they are on duty, which is really what I'm looking into," Bergstrom told Jason. "People can do a lot of things off duty, whether they are good or bad, as long as they don't transpire into the workplace. And it sounds like from what you are telling me that everything you know happened outside of work." Bergstrom was looking for evidence that Shad and I had hooked up while on duty, which we never had and which we never would.

After that meeting with Bergstrom, the union rep who sat

in on it with me was reassuring. He said Bergstrom was trying to convey to us that this investigation was nothing to be worried about. Bergstrom said as much several days later when he supposedly wrote Shad an email saying Shad shouldn't "worry about it too much." Others downplayed it as well. Shad told me he went to Captain Moore and told him that he was worried that I would lose my job "over a crazy letter written by a crazy person." Moore said, "Well, that's not going to happen, but if it did, there is nothing you could do about it."

Bergstrom did what Snow asked and examined our officer history records for nine days between May 12 and May 21. While I was preparing my rebuttal letter to Chief Hahn, I determined that I worked eleven days in the month of May and that Shad and I exchanged calls on five of those days.

Bergstrom's report:

Officer Perez's history showed that she was active all shift, either on self-initiated activity (she ran over fifty license plates on her mobile data computer, indicating she was conducting some type of activity) or she ran mostly call to call with a few breaks in between calls for service.

The average number of minutes for those calls over the five days was fifteen minutes per day. I explained this to Hahn in my letter to him. Is that a lot? I don't know. Neither did Bergstrom. To know whether that's a high number, you have to know what *all* the officers are doing. For all we know, spending fifteen minutes on personal calls in an eleven-hour shift might be extremely low.

According to Bergstrom's report:

> The department policy is not specific to the amount of time one can make a personal phone call while on duty, just that they cannot undertake activities that impact their ability to perform their job as a peace officer efficiently…The overall review of the policy would then suggest that the officers must not interfere in their work performance as a result of making personal calls but that the occasional personal call of short duration is acceptable.

Although it was not Bergstrom's job to reach a conclusion about whether Shad and I had shirked our duties, he pointed out that most of the time, our calls were brief. The only exceptions were May 12, when I was on vacation, and on May 20, when we had seven calls for a total of forty-three minutes over an eleven-hour shift. I was never asked the reasons for the phone calls or if any of them had happened during a break. And even on days when we talked, we were very busy with police work. Bergstrom mentions that a couple of times in his report.

When Bergstrom looked at Eleanor Mann's distorted accusations more closely, it seemed clear they didn't hold any water. Yes, Shad and I started a relationship after we split from our spouses. No, we did not have sex while on duty. No, we did not spend an inordinate amount of time talking on our personal cell phones and texting back and forth. In fact, Shad and I seemed to be going out of our way to keep our personal calls tucked away in the quiet corners of otherwise busy workdays. So, we should be exonerated, right?

Not so fast.

LIEUTENANT CALVIN WALSTAD TAKES OVER

Bergstrom didn't have the power to make any decisions on our case. He passed all the information from his interviews on to Lieutenant Calvin Walstad, who wrote up the investigation and his opinion on the next course of action. From there, Walstad's findings would go to Captain Moore. Ultimately, it was Moore who would determine the punishment, based on Walstad's recommendations, which were based on Bergstrom's information. Bergstrom may have said it was all no big deal, but in reality, he had no idea what decisions would ultimately be made at the end of this chain of command.

Walstad's job was to determine if I had an unsatisfactory work performance that included incompetence, inefficiency, or delay in performing. He was also asked to determine if I had engaged in any conduct "which the employee knows or reasonably should know is unbecoming (a police officer) or which is contrary to good order, efficiency, or morale, or which tends to reflect unfavorably upon the department or its members." These were the two policies filed against Shad and me, based on Bergstrom's report.

Since no one had ever accused me of being an incompetent officer, and Bergstrom's own report found no evidence of violating the listed policies between Shad and me, a reasonable person would conclude that these charges were bogus and should not be upheld. That's certainly what Shad and I thought.

It's not what Walstad thought, however.

Walstad filed his recommendations ten days after being assigned to my case on July 1. In my mind, his report was a mixture of moralistic sermonizing and blatant contradictions.

He sustained both charges against me. For the first allegation—of being incompetent and inefficient in carrying out orders—he focused on one call I had with Shad while driving to the Foothills Tennis Village to investigate a noise complaint. Another instance he cited was a call Shad and I had after I had conducted an area check looking for a suspicious vehicle. Another one Walstad noted was a thirteen-minute call we had while I was on an early morning foot patrol at a shopping area.

A word on police work here: In order to be efficient workers, police officers must master the ability to multitask. When a citizen calls to report a loud noise, I am capable of holding a quiet, short conversation on my phone while I drive around the neighborhood (or just sit in my patrol vehicle) listening for loud noises. I am also capable of holding a conversation while out on foot patrols in general. Police officers are expected to spend time in their "beat," or the area of town in which they work, and our superiors didn't want to see us at the police station. It's to be expected that during an eleven-hour shift, life happens...I have to take a phone call or use the restroom at times when there's nothing going on in my beat. I would often self-initiate a foot patrol in order to squeeze in a bathroom break. This allowed me to radio in my location, for my own safety, without announcing over the radio that I was using the bathroom. But this kind of practice was held against me when I self-initiated a foot patrol and took a call at the same time.

Despite going into a detailed analysis of these calls and where I was located at the time, Walstad concluded, "It is unknown if Officer Perez being on the telephone delayed her response to the call for service."

No evidence? Well, let's find her guilty anyway.

On the second charge, he dispensed with factual evidence altogether and sustained the allegation that my behavior was unbecoming by claiming my relationship with Shad was "unprofessional." He claimed we tried to keep the relationship secret, which "reflects unfavorably upon the Roseville Police Department," and noted that Shad and I were both "married and have small children." He didn't mention that we were both separated, and he brought our kids into it, even though that was never a part of the investigation.

He also declared our relationship "put other officers on their shift at risk." This one was particularly perplexing because I didn't see the connection between me dating Shad and our fellow officers' personal safety. No one ever raised that as an issue. I had an excellent officer safety record, and I would never put anyone else at risk. Shad and I never did anything inappropriate while on duty. We didn't secretly meet. We got together with friends. We went to dinner in public. We weren't hiding out.

To understand Walstad's report, it helps to understand the lieutenant's relationship with Shad. Walstad saw Shad like a son. Walstad's son had been in the military, like Shad, and the two had bonded over that. Walstad considered Shad a friend, and I think he was offended that Shad hadn't told him about his relationship with me. This might explain why, despite there being no rule stating that Shad and I should have informed anyone about our relationship, Walstad decided to judge us on this point in his report.

"I would have expected officers Begley and Perez to notify their sergeant and/or lieutenant to advise they are involved in a personal relationship so they could be assigned to different patrol shifts," Walstad wrote in the report. But in depositions, he admitted this wasn't standard protocol:

> Lawyer: Is it stated anywhere in policy that they must report a romantic relationship to their supervisor?
>
> Walstad: It is not on a peer level. It is on a supervisor level, but it is not on a peer level.

Department policy stated that if a supervisor was dating an officer, the relationship must be reported. But fellow officers who were dating were not required to report their relationship or be separated to different patrol shifts. Walstad was making this "rule" up on the spot.

Walstad didn't know Shad and Eleanor were separated. Later, when my attorney took his deposition, Walstad admitted that being aware of Shad's separation would have "made a difference" in his review of the IA investigation. When asked if he had any "personal feelings" about this case, he said, "I feel their relationship was inappropriate."

Not only does this seemingly betray that Walstad was making moral appraisals about our relationship, it's directly contrary to what Bergstrom told us when he started his IA investigation. Bergstrom said he was not investigating our relationship. He was only investigating whether anything inappropriate happened while we were on duty. But then here comes Walstad, making all sorts of moral appraisals and admitting he was drawing conclusions based on his personal beliefs.

However, in his deposition, Walstad later admitted he was aware of other officers who conducted extramarital affairs "while on duty."

> Lawyer: Do you have any information that any officers at the Roseville Police Department engaged in extramarital affairs other than officers Begley and Perez?
>
> Walstad: Yes.
>
> Lawyer: Did any of those other extramarital affairs occur while officers were on duty?
>
> Walstad: Yes.
>
> Lawyer: You said, when asked about your personal feelings, you felt that the relationship was inappropriate. My question

is: Why? Why did you come to the conclusion that it was inappropriate, specifically?

Walstad: Both of them were married. Both of them had young children at the time. I also felt—or I also feel that if I have safety concerns when there's two officers who are involved in a relationship that work on the same shift or the same side of patrol. Those are my personal feelings.

Lawyer: Did you ever inquire into the status of Officer Begley or Officer Perez's marriages at the time?

Walstad: I did not.

Lawyer: So you had no understanding that Officer Perez was separated at the time?

Walstad: I did not.

Lawyer: Would that have made a difference in your review of the internal affairs investigation?

Walstad: It would.

Walstad wrote up his judgments and delivered them to Captain Moore—without checking with Shad or me whether his understanding was correct.

Lawyer: With respect to Ms. Perez, you really didn't know what her marital status was, did you?

Walstad: No, sir, not at the time.

Lawyer: Yet you wrote it in your part of your analysis sustaining this allegation, right?

Roseville Lawyer: Well, argumentative. He said he had an understanding.

Lawyer: Well, the document speaks for itself. You wrote it there, so it must have been significant to you, right?

Walstad: Yes, sir.

Lawyer: Now, normally in your practice, in your career, and significant issues like that, I'm assuming you would base those on some foundation of fact, correct?

Walstad: Yes, sir.

Lawyer: Yet, in this case, you did not with respect to Ms. Perez, right?

Roseville Lawyer: Objection. Argumentative. It misstates his testimony. Go ahead.

Walstad: You are correct. I did not have the complete facts in regards to her marital status at the time.

At a separate point in the deposition, Walstad noted that he felt my relationship with Shad was "inappropriate."

Walstad: If they're both married at the time, it was inappropriate for the extramarital affair.

Lawyer: That's more of a moral decision, right? That's not a departmental operational decision?

Walstad: Correct. Correct. But it would be with the codes of ethics, unethical behavior.

Lawyer: What part of it is unethical in a law enforcement context under the law enforcement code about this?

Walstad: Both are married. They've given their commitment to another, and yet they're in a relationship with someone else.

Lawyer: I'm just trying to get my head around this. What if one or both of those individuals while legally married were separated, does that change your analysis at all?

Walstad: It would.

Lawyer: In doing your evaluation, when you reviewed Lieutenant Bergstrom's report, understanding the importance of what we're just talking about here, that would have been a good fact to know, right?

Walstad: Yes, sir, it would have been.

About two months after Bergstrom's investigative report was issued, Moore released his findings, which were based on Walstad's report. He found that both charges against Shad and me had been sustained.

THE MEMORANDUM I REFUSED TO SIGN

When the IA investigation concluded, I was called into Captain Moore's office the morning of August 23. Lieutenant Marc Glynn was already in Moore's office, sitting in a chair at the back of the room. I sat down in the empty chair in front of the captain's desk.

Moore slid a piece of paper across the desk to me and asked me to read it.

The document was a memorandum from Captain Moore to me, stating that I was receiving a written reprimand for violation of two sections of the Roseville Police Department Policy Manual. The first violation was "unsatisfactory work performance," and the second was "any other on-duty or off-duty conduct which any employee knows or reasonably should know is unbecoming a member of the department."

Moore's memo listed the grounds for each violation. To support the "unsatisfactory work performance" claim, there was a list of calls between Shad and me—the list Bergstrom had gotten from Eleanor Mann.

As far as I knew, I was a good cop. And when Moore was deposed, he also acknowledged that I performed well as an officer (even if it took him a moment to remember).

> Lawyer: So around this time that this Lieutenant Richardson and Sergeant Morris gave you this information [about Perez's attitude], did you have any understanding of how Officer Perez's job performance was?
>
> Moore: I don't recall.
>
> Lawyer: The information that I've gathered in this case, I can just represent to you, has been that at least on her abilities to perform the job, she appeared to do that fairly well. Was that your impression?
>
> Moore: Yes, I would say that characterizes my impression of her at the time as well.

When I was on duty, I didn't wait around for a call. I was

proactive and stayed busy. I would never put off responding to a call so I could finish chatting with my boyfriend. I took police work seriously, and I had years of experience working in places much tougher than Roseville, California. Nothing in the IA investigation had shown I had shirked my duties or performed poorly. In fact, all of my evaluations had been excellent.

As I read through Moore's document, I became upset. I was afraid of losing my job—not because I agreed with the violations or thought it would be possible to lose my job over an off-duty relationship, but because I kept thinking about what my dad had said: that while I was on probation, the department didn't need a reason to fire me. Since Jason and I had separated, I needed my own income to survive and provide for my two kids. But I became most angry when I read the last paragraph of the allegations.

"You failed to keep your relationship with Shad Begley, a married coworker, separate from your employment, as evidenced by the previously mentioned phone usage that you both admit was personal in nature," the memo read. A few lines later, Moore wrote that my relationship with Shad "ultimately reflected negatively on the department."

Upon reading this, I was incensed. Bergstrom had explicitly upheld that our on-duty behavior was being investigated, not our relationship. He even asserted this in his deposition for my case against the city:

> Lawyer: During your investigation, did you ever investigate the marital status of Officer Begley?
>
> Bergstrom: No.
>
> Lawyer: Was it important to your investigation what Officer Perez's marital status was at the time?
>
> Bergstrom: No.

Yet here it was in print on Moore's memorandum: My relationship with a "married" coworker was deemed inappropriate.

> Lawyer: Why did it matter whether they were married?
>
> Moore: I think that it put into question whether or not them carrying on the relationship at work was appropriate or not.
>
> Lawyer: Okay. But there's no information to suggest that they were carrying on any part of the relationship at work other than communicating with each other, right?
>
> Moore: Correct.

Lawyer: [...] That investigation did not find that they committed any interaction other than talking on the phone or texting on the telephone, right?

Moore: Correct.

Lawyer: Okay. So again, do you think it is relevant to consider the marital status of an officer with this type of investigation?

Moore: No. I'm sorry.

Moore clearly didn't know Shad and I were both separated from our spouses, and he was making a moral call that was about to impact my career.

At the end of the document, there was a line for me to sign.

I looked up from the page. "I don't agree with this," I said.

Moore gave me a hard stare. I suddenly had a surge of courage. I'd received positive feedback on my work performance from my superiors. I kept my work calls and personal calls separate, and my personal cell phone use was typical of everyone else I'd seen in the department. Shad and I had both separated from our spouses, and there were no policies preventing fellow officers from dating. The violations Moore listed weren't accurate or fair.

Looking at these violations, I simply did not feel free to live my personal life the way I wanted to. If the same scenario had happened when I was younger, in my twenties, I might have rolled over and signed the document, walked out of the room, and never looked back. But in my thirties, I was beyond the point of agreeing to something that was wrong.

Moore waited.

"Are you ordering me to sign it?" I asked. "Because if you are, I will sign it. I don't want to be insubordinate. But if you're not ordering me to sign it, I'm not going to sign it because I don't agree that I violated these two policies."

"I'm not ordering you to sign it," Moore said.

"Then I'm not going to sign," I replied.

By the look on his face, I got the impression that Moore was not used to being told no, especially not by a female officer on probation.

On the signature line at the bottom of the document, Moore wrote, "Refused." Then he told me I needed to set up a meeting with Chief Hahn to talk about it.

I was scared. I wasn't sure what would happen when I crossed Captain Moore.

CHAPTER 3

FIGHTING THE ACCUSATIONS

Shad and I both appealed our written reprimands. This allowed me an administrative hearing before Chief Hahn. My hearing was scheduled for September 4.

In addition to Captain Moore's written reprimand, I also read the recommendations Lieutenant Walstad had prepared for Moore after reviewing Bergstrom's investigation. Walstad never interviewed Shad or me; he created his memo solely from the information Bergstrom provided to him. It was Walstad's analysis that ultimately informed Moore's reprimand. I sorted through the assertions in Walstad's memo as I prepared my rebuttal for Chief Hahn.

I explained that the investigation had shown that I hadn't violated the policies in question. For the first, "unsatisfactory work performance," Walstad had noted the list of phone calls between Shad and me from a single day that stuck out to him as being unusual. But he noted that he was unable to come to a conclusion as to whether the calls affected my performance. It was acceptable for officers to use their personal cell phones while on breaks or when there was a necessary circumstance. I'd carried out all my regular duties in a timely manner. Not only was there no evidence that the calls had interfered with my work, but Bergstrom never asked during the investigation what my reasons were for the calls that day, or what Shad and I talked about. Walstad was trying to assess whether I'd violated a policy on "unsatisfactory work performance...without a reasonable and bona fide excuse." How could the alleged violation be sustained, I wrote, when a reasonable and bona fide excuse was never asked for?

On the second violation, for conduct unbecoming a member of the department, Walstad had written in his report that our relationship, "because of being secret in nature," was unprofessional. This statement was an unfounded judgment on Walstad's part. Shad and I didn't hide our relationship in any way; we'd gone grocery shopping and run errands together in public. Further down in Walstad's report, he wrote that "both officers are married with young children," which seemed to indicate Walstad's moral bias. The fact that Shad and I each had young children was irrelevant. As for our marriages, they were each in the beginning stages of divorce.

Walstad also wrote that he would have expected Shad and me to notify our superiors of our relationship, so we could be put on different patrol shifts. There was a policy in place that dating coworkers must be on different shifts if one was a superior but Shad and I held the same rank. There was no policy indicating we had an obligation to tell anyone about our relationship or that we were required to work separate shifts. This note of Walstad's was a telling one: He wasn't holding me to a specific policy, but to his own expectations. It was inappropriate for the department to discipline me for Walstad's personal beliefs.

I wrote down these arguments in my rebuttal to Chief Hahn and asserted that it was obvious I hadn't violated the two policy sections that had been sustained. Bergstrom's investigation didn't support the two violations Walstad had plucked for his report. "The only thing I may have violated," I continued, "is the personal, moral beliefs of one or more Roseville Police supervisors."

In my meeting with Chief Hahn, I intended to present a strong case for why the allegations against me should not have been sustained.

A HOSTILE ENVIRONMENT

While I waited for my administrative hearing, I felt like a pariah around the station. One day I ran into Sergeant Winston Slate in the breakroom and said hello. He just looked at me and said nothing. The same thing happened one day in the locker room when Sergeant Morris also ignored me.

The clear aversion I saw from my superiors got so bad that I looked up the department's policy on discriminatory harassment. It stated that harassment is any verbal or physical conduct that demeans or shows hostility or aversion toward an individual based upon that individual's protected class. I felt that I was being treated in a hostile fashion based on my marital status. Was that a protected class?

Yes, it was.

A good example of that discrimination was when Shad and I tried to do a shift trade.

On August 29, I was very sick, and Shad said he would work my shift for me. He called Sergeant Hugo Howard and told him about the shift change. Howard said he'd put it on the schedule.

I'd never done a shift trade in Roseville before, but I knew officers made shift trades all the time and that there wasn't a policy about them. You simply filled out a form, and the two officers changing their shifts signed it and turned it in to the desk sergeant.

Shad assured me he'd never had an issue with shift trades before. Half the time, no one bothered filling out the form. Sometimes, the replacement officer merely showed up at the shift briefing, and no one cared or said anything. "As long as there's a body in the briefing," Shad said, "it doesn't matter."

Informally, when shifts were traded, they were supposed to be "paid back," so that each officer works one shift for the other. I reviewed the calendars, and they showed that Shad had traded shifts with a male officer in March and that Shad never paid the officer back. The system seemed pretty loose. I was used to that from my time in the South San Francisco police department. If you did a shift trade with somebody, you could pay them back right away or down the road. It was up to the two officers.

When I didn't feel better after a few days, we tried to do a second shift trade. Shad told me not to worry about paying him back right away. He called to tell the shift sergeant, Kelby Newton, who advised Shad that I had to repay the first trade within the next few days. Otherwise, I would be short hours, and Shad would have to get overtime.

Neither Shad nor I had heard about this rule, so I got in

contact with Newton. I remember the call well. I was sitting on the floor of my bedroom, feeling terrible.

During the conversation, I asked Newton, "What is the policy and procedure for a shift trade?"

The sergeant admitted he could not find an actual written policy. Then he launched into a long and involved explanation about pay periods and my hours being short and the need for me to pay Shad back over the next three days.

"I can't do that," I told him. "I'm very sick."

And I know Newton could *tell* I was sick. I was congested and had a croaking voice. During the call, I actually had to lay down on the floor because I was so sick.

"I'm just explaining what the rules are," Newton said. Then he said he was eating lunch and would need to call me back.

Much later, when we took his deposition, Newton said he spoke with Lieutenant Glynn about shift trades. They did some research and couldn't find a formal policy on shift trades. The only rules they could find was on the shift trade form itself, which said that "typically the trade will be completed in the same pay period." But he and Glynn decided that if I was sick, I could wait until the next pay period to cover the shift I owed to Shad. He called me back and told me this, and I told him I'd look at my calendar and get back to him about the day I would work for Shad.

When I got off the phone, I took a deep breath and tried to collect my thoughts. I was feeling terribly beaten down. My marriage had fallen apart, and my supervisors had called me immoral. I'd been given a written reprimand accusing me of unsatisfactory work performance and behavior that brought shame to the entire police force. Everything I did was being put under a microscope. I couldn't even do a simple shift trade without sergeants and lieutenants challenging me.

Shift trades were routine for most officers—the men, mostly it seemed—but when I needed to do one, suddenly there's red tape and complications. Why? Was it because I was a woman? I'd never doubted my abilities as a police officer before, but I began to doubt whether I could continue working for the Roseville Police Department.

I thought of Asher Martin making rude hand gestures in the briefing, or a sergeant, Howard, who'd allegedly slapped a female civilian on the buttocks while she was on a ride-along. Shad had told me Howard hadn't been demoted for that behavior. Even Shad yelled at Lieutenant Bergstrom at the conclusion of the IA investigation (an incident I'll describe in more depth later on). Guys like Shad, Asher, Howard, and everyone else just do what they want, but when I tried to arrange a simple shift trade, my request was scrutinized. I wanted to know why.

I talked to Newton again later in the day. "Have I done something to tick you off?" Newton said.

Maybe he was asking me this because he could tell I was ill or maybe because I was just simply asking questions, but I never yelled. I never so much as raised my voice. I was not rude. I know that for a fact. I respect supervisors. I was very sick, but there was no way I would cross the line and say something disrespectful.

I hadn't worked with Newton before. I didn't know him that well. But he seemed part of this group of bullies who enjoyed using rules and regulations to hassle people they didn't want around. I told him that I was being singled out because of my relationship with Shad and that we were being treated differently.

"I've never had a problem with you before," Newton said.

"I'm not trying to cause a problem," I assured him.

"I'm just the middle-man here," Newton said. "I'm just passing along what Lieutenant Glynn told me. The shift has to be paid back during the same pay period. That's the policy."

I had heard Newton had a tarnished history with the Roseville Police Department. In 2010, three officers had filed a civil rights lawsuit against the department claiming the department's officers had fostered a hostile work environment that targeted gay officers and those perceived to be gay. The incidents they cited went back several years, and Newton was one of the defendants. He'd been accused of making homophobic comments to a straight police officer about that officer's relationship with a gay officer.

I wasn't there at the time, but according to the local newspaper that covered the lawsuit, sexually discriminatory harassment was commonplace in the Roseville Police Department.[1] Newton was one of three defendants. The others were the former police chief Mike Blair and Roseville City Manager Craig Robinson. Eventually, the case was settled without any admission of wrongdoing, and the officers were paid $490,000.[2] Blair and Robinson were both gone, but Newton had kept his job.

Years later, after I had sued the department, the city's lawyers suggested that I was being belligerent with Newton and trying to get out of my work responsibilities. That wasn't true. I was merely asking Newton why he was enforcing a time limit on the trade involving me while others paid back

---

1 Jon Brines, "Details Released in Roseville Police Anti-Gay Harassment Lawsuit," *Gold Country Media*, February 18, 2010.

2 Jon Brines, "Roseville Settles Civil Rights Case for $490,000," *Gold Country Media*, May 13, 2011.

their trades whenever it was convenient for them. Why was I being singled out this way?

"Listen," I said finally to Newton. "This is getting too complicated. I'll just take sick time."

That should have been the end of it, but it wasn't.

THE SECRET MEMO

After he and I talked, Newton was summoned to a meeting. Newton was surprised to find Chief Hahn, Captain Moore, and Lieutenant Glynn waiting for him. They asked him about the call with me and then told him to write up a memo recounting the conversation we'd had.

Newton later admitted the request struck him as odd. "I don't think I've ever memorialized a phone conversation before," he told my attorney in his deposition.

Newton said he wasn't aware of an IA investigation into Shad and me, and he didn't know me to be a troublemaker. He said he had only supervised me a couple of times but that he remembered that I was "very quiet" but also a "good employee."

"I never heard her talk like that before," Newton said, recounting the questions I raised about the shift-trade policy. "I think my speculation is she was frustrated with the situation, and it could have been that she was sick too on top of it."

But Newton's memo portrayed me as much more than sick and frustrated. He described me as being "agitated" in our calls. He said I was unhappy about things in the department. He said I was irritated.

Later, when we took Newton's deposition, his tone was throttled back significantly. Perhaps I wasn't angry after all. Maybe he had just *interpreted* how I felt.

"It kind of *seemed* like she was agitated about the situation," Newton clarified in his deposition. "It was more like tone of voice. She wasn't yelling or screaming or saying vulgarities or nothing like that. It was just, you can tell when someone is maybe a little bit more..."

At that point in his deposition, Newton's voice trailed off and he stopped talking. It seemed to me he was close to admitting I'd been mischaracterized in his memo, but he never finished his thought.

Let's step back for a moment and look at what's going on here.

Here's a guy, Newton, who was recently sued for fostering

a sexually discriminating environment in the police department. He gets called into the police chief's office, and his captain and his lieutenant are there with the chief, and they are looking for any proof they can gin up that this probationary officer is a malcontent. They want written proof of how disruptive I am. So they tell Newton to write a memo about his conversation with me.

What's he going to do? My guess is that he decided to give them what they wanted, whether it was true or not. So he made sure I sounded argumentative and defiant.

CHIEF HAHN AND THE APPEAL HEARING

Despite my lingering illness and the hassles I faced over my shift trade with Shad, I spent several hours in late August and early September working on my rebuttal to the written reprimand. Although I was ostracized at work and thought my career in Roseville had taken a possibly irreversible beating in the last two months, I also felt that I had a strong case. I felt that once Chief Hahn heard my side of the story, he would agree that I had done nothing wrong and would rescind Moore's written reprimand.

They would see that it was all a big mistake.

It was not an illicit affair. It was merely a case of two officers dating and helping each other through a difficult period.

It was not secretive. Shad and I had merely done a good job of staying professional while on the job.

We were not shirking our duties. We'd made a few personal calls, it's true. But so did everyone else. We hadn't violated any department policies, and we executed our responsibilities efficiently and professionally.

The allegations against us were based on exaggerated claims and false accusations, and the investigation into those allegations had been too narrowly focused to prove anything.

They'd see they owed me an apology.

Although I'd written a detailed rebuttal, I was nervous going into the meeting with Hahn. He is not what you'd describe as a warm or engaging individual. He struck me as stiff and somewhat cold, which didn't help my nerves at all. Still, I was confident that if I presented my case thoroughly, Hahn would agree to rescind the written reprimand. I was good at my job, and I'd done great work in Roseville. Hahn had written notes to me praising me for how good I was doing.

When I met with Hahn on September 4, I gave my verbal rebuttal. I used some strong language, I talked about being discriminated against, and from time to time, I felt myself getting emotional.

Hahn sat there in silence. He seemed to be listening, but I could not tell if I was getting through to him. He asked a couple of questions, such as, "Why do you specifically feel like you were discriminated against?" But I did most of the talking for the thirty-minute session, and when I was done, I thought I'd made a strong, reasonable case that I had done nothing wrong and had been victimized by false accusations and the bias of Hahn's officers.

When I was finished, Hahn handed me a piece of paper.

"This is for you," he said. "I'm releasing you from probation."

I looked at the paper. It was a termination letter. I was stunned. I had no idea I would be fired at this meeting. It hadn't even crossed my mind. I handed the letter to my union rep, who'd come into the meeting with me. He looked shocked.

> 3.06.170 Release of Probationer. During an Employee's initial probationary period, an Employee may be released from City service without cause at the sole discretion of the City. Such release shall not be subject to any appeal. Notification of release in writing shall be provided to the probationer, and a copy filed with the Director. (Ord. 3213 § 1 (part), 1998.).
>
> You are being released because you did not successfully complete your probationary period. You are responsible for returning all city property.

We wish you luck in future endeavors.

"Why?" I asked Hahn. "Why are you releasing me from probation?"

"I don't have to provide you with that information," Hahn said.

And that was it. In the end, my dad had been right.

I left the room and was greeted by Lieutenants Glynn and Richardson. I'd seen these two lurking around outside the meeting room before my session with Hahn. That should have tipped me off as to what was about to happen. Glynn and Richardson escorted me to the locker room so I could clear out my locker and collect all my other stuff. On my way out, I passed the union rep. He didn't say anything, but he gave me this sad, puppy-dog look.

I was angry with everybody. Shad had been writing me emails saying how he'd stand up for me, but where was he now? I was angry at Jason. If he hadn't called Eleanor that night, none of this would have happened. No IA investigation. No written reprimand. No termination. I called him. "You just had to get that Eleanor involved, didn't you? You're the reason I lost my job. You caused this!"

I also blamed myself. I'm a person who takes responsibility

for their mistakes. Maybe there was a better way to go about seeing Shad. I could have waited until my probation was over. I could have just signed the written reprimand Moore had handed me and moved on.

But I didn't. There was never any inappropriate behavior between us on duty. Who I have a relationship with off duty is my own business and not my employer's. They can't control my life. They shouldn't be free to reprimand me when I've done nothing wrong.

Perhaps the biggest mistake I made was standing up for myself. This only pissed them off. Clearly, they didn't like a thirty-something female patrol officer pushing back and telling them that they'd made a mistake. To them, I became a problem, and they got rid of me as a result.

As for the big deal that was made over the shift trade? I've had years to replay everything in my mind, and I think the real reason my shift trade request was scrutinized was because Moore and Hahn had already decided to fire me. No female was going to walk into this department and refuse Captain Moore without a serious consequence. They didn't want me to trade a shift I would never pay back. Of course, they would ask Newton to document his conversation with me because then the shift trade could become a convenient scapegoat for the termination they had already planned.

I fell into a terrible depression. I was angry. Full of regret. Humiliated. A little while after my meeting with Hahn, I heard that one of the Roseville motorcycle cops was telling people that I was fired for having sex with Shad in the back seat of a patrol car. I couldn't bring myself to interview for another police job. How would I explain what happened? How am I going to explain to an interview panel why I was released from probation? What could I say? I didn't even know why I was released. The chief never gave me a reason. I'm assuming at that point that I was fired for having a relationship with a fellow cop, and I couldn't imagine having to talk about any of this with someone from another police force. I also was well aware of how well-connected other agencies are with each other. I knew Lieutenant Richardson was married to a captain in the police department in a neighboring city. I was just too embarrassed.

This was one of the lowest points in my life. I had lost my career, and I had no confidence that I could get back into it.

But, as it turns out, the Roseville Police Department wasn't done with me yet.

CHAPTER 4

THE COVER-UP

It's incredibly difficult to tease apart exactly why I was terminated. I think that is by design.

When depositions began for my lawsuit against the City of Roseville, Hahn, Moore, and Walstad in 2014—and we'll get to that case soon—Hahn initially said he didn't agree with the findings in the IA investigation.

> Lawyer: Drawing your attention to the second page, Lieutenant Walstad sustains a violation of section 340.35(c), essentially unsatisfactory work performance for a variety of things and describes Officer Perez's use of the telephone and interaction with Officer Begley. Did you agree with his finding to sustain that particular charge?
>
> Roseville Lawyer: Just for the purposes of clarity of the record, I am going to object that it misstates a little bit of what the

document says, which lists recommendations of these findings. So with that, go ahead and answer.

Hahn: No, I did not.

Lawyer: Why not?

Hahn: [...] I didn't see anything in the internal affairs report that could prove [...] that something didn't get done that should have got done.

Lawyer: Then drawing attention to the next allegation. The next allegation was a violation of section 340.3.5(aa), which describes any other on-duty or off-duty conduct which any employee knows or reasonably should know to be unbecoming a member of the department that is contrary to good order, efficiency or morale or tends to reflect unfavorably on the department's members, Lieutenant Walstad then recommending sustaining that particular allegation. Did you agree with his recommendation in this regard?

Hahn: No, I did not.

Lawyer: Why not?

Hahn: Well, one, a lot of allegations in the original complaint were things happening on duty, and none of those were proven that they happened on duty. So now we're just dealing with off-duty conduct, and I didn't see any off-duty conduct that affected morale or standing of the department kind of thing.

My lawyer went on to remind him of Walstad's description that my relationship with Shad "because of being secret, reflects unfavorably upon the Roseville Police Department and its members." He also pointed to where Walstad noted that we were each "married with young children."

> Lawyer: Did that fact have anything to do with your decision-making with respect to Ms. Perez, the fact that she was involved in a relationship with Officer Begley and one or both of them were married at the time? Did that—
>
> Hahn: Which decision? You said—
>
> Lawyer: Your decision to terminate her?
>
> Hahn: No. Absolutely not.
>
> Lawyer: That didn't factor in any way?
>
> Hahn: No.
>
> Lawyer: You didn't agree with this recommendation, either?
>
> Hahn: Correct.

> Lawyer: So did ultimately, this internal affairs investigation, did it come to you?
>
> Hahn: After the discipline, yes, it comes to me, and I'm the admin hearing officer. So the discipline of which was ultimately a letter of reprimand came from the captain [Moore], and then the administrative hearing officer is myself.

For a while, as I was sorting through this case and its aftermath, I believed that Moore was ultimately the one who disciplined me with the letter of reprimand and that Hahn didn't hear of the results of the IA investigation until it was over—just like Hahn said in his deposition. But when Walstad was deposed, he painted the story differently.

> Lawyer: Did he [Chief Hahn] indicate to you what his decision would be in regard to Officer Perez?
>
> Walstad: Yes.
>
> Lawyer: What did he indicate to you?
>
> Walstad: That both Officers Perez and Begley would receive a written reprimand in regard to the investigation.

According to Walstad, Hahn knew about the discipline Shad and I were to receive as a result of the IA investigation. And in my mind, if Hahn really did know that I would be getting a written reprimand, I must assume that he at least agreed with it at that point in time; otherwise, why would he have allowed me to receive it?

Later in his deposition, Hahn also claimed that talking on the cell phone was also not a factor in his decision to terminate me.

> Hahn: And I just thought that when you boil down the internal affairs complaint, it boils down to talking on the phone. Did I really want to release somebody...if really all it was, was talking on the phone? And so that's why I did not release her at the time.

And yet, not long after this statement, Hahn completely backtracked, saying his decision to fire me had hinged in part on the IA investigation.

> Lawyer: Why did you terminate Janelle?

> Hahn: There were multiple things that happened in a short period of time that led me to believe that Ms. Perez would not be a good fit for our police department.

> Lawyer: What were those things?

> Hahn: Well, first was the internal affairs case where another officer's wife complained that there was inappropriate behav-

ior happening on duty between her husband and Janelle. That case ran its course and got resolved.

Hahn's claim that the case was "resolved" was completely inaccurate. The IA investigation wasn't resolved at the time I'd been fired—remember, at our last meeting, I delivered my rebuttal to the moralistic findings against me, and *that's* when Hahn handed me the letter of termination. He'd made the decision before the investigation had closed. And at another point when my lawyer pressed him on whether the IA investigation was a factor in his decision to terminate me, he admitted it plainly.

> Lawyer: So it would be fair for me to say [...] that the whole Eleanor Mann complaint, internal affairs investigation, all of that, didn't have anything to do with your decision to terminate Ms. Perez?
>
> Hahn: No. I would say it was part of it.

And as for the "multiple things" that apparently happened to push Hahn to the final decision? Those were even more obscure. Sometime after Walstad filed his recommendations and before my appeal hearing, Hahn asked his officers to find out what kind of officer I was. And an important note here: Hahn did not ask officers to report on Shad's productivity. This additional scrutiny was reserved just for me.

Lawyer: Did you request or did you receive similar [performance and productivity] information for Officer Begley?

Hahn: I did not.

Lawyer: Why not?

Hahn: Because he's not on probation. He wasn't in training.

Lawyer: But he was under investigation as well regarding this complaint that was made by his then-wife, right?

Hahn: Correct.

When the supervisors took the time to look at my actions and my performance—to do an actual investigation where they analyzed facts and talked to both sides—they found that I did nothing wrong. In fact, they learned I was a pretty good officer. I had excellent evaluations, and there was no indication that I ever let my personal life interfere with my police work. Although a productivity investigation by Lieutenant Glynn revealed that my numbers were "average to above average," Hahn said three other issues came up during this time. The first came from Lieutenant Richardson, who apparently claimed some of the department's female officers had raised concerns about my attitude and poor communications with them. In his deposition, Hahn was unclear about the details of this claim.

Hahn: Shortly after that investigation was done, one of my lieutenants [Lieutenant Richardson] said that there were some other officers questioning Janelle and her attitude and there was some sort of perceived, I don't remember exactly what they said, but some sort of, 'What's wrong with her? Why isn't she communicating with us?' kind of thing.

Another issue was raised by Bergstrom, who said a woman from a domestic violence incident had called to say I had been rude. The woman declined to file a complaint, however. I was never notified of the call or given feedback about this encounter.

The straw that broke the camel's back, Hahn later said, was when Newton had reported the details of my shift trade call with him, the day I was home sick on the floor of my bedroom. Newton said I'd exhibited a bad attitude. That, combined with the unnamed domestic violence complaint and the vague concerns of Richardson, was reason enough to let me go, Hahn decided.

So, in the end, my termination had nothing to do with dating Shad, Hahn claimed. It had nothing to do with the phone calls or the IA investigation—even though ironically, these are the first considerations Hahn brought up when my lawyer originally asked why he'd terminated me. My termination had nothing to do with work performance.

Instead, he fell back on this new "evidence" that had emerged concerning my "agitated" calls with Newton, the complaints from other female officers, and the "angry" domestic violence complaint. None of these incidents had been part of an IA investigation. In fact, there was no investigation into these claims at all. No one formally interviewed the other female police officers about me. No one interviewed the domestic violence complainant. No one interviewed me about my conversation with Sergeant Newton.

In fact, it wasn't until Hahn's deposition that I learned about the flimsy complaints that led to my termination. Why had they been willing to spend weeks investigating my phone calls with Shad but had taken these other allegations at face value? Were they worried that if they investigated that these new allegations would be as weak as the previous ones leveled by Eleanor Mann?

Here's what I think really happened: Hahn looked at the IA investigation, initially agreed with its moralistic findings, and told Captain Moore to issue punishment to Shad and me in the form of written reprimands. I didn't just roll over and take mine. When I refused to sign that document, I think it sent them all spinning, and it sealed my fate. Chief Hahn realized there was no legal ground to stand on to discipline me over Walstad's and Moore's moral accusations, and he began looking for any other possible excuse to bury me.

AN UNDERHANDED TRICK

Let's take a closer look at that memo from Newton—the one that he'd been requested to write outside of standard protocol and which had been quietly slipped into my file without notice.

I didn't become aware of the Newton memo in my file until around March 2014, when I requested a copy of my file to prepare questions for legal depositions in my lawsuit against the city. I was shocked to read the memo. Not only had I been unaware of it, but no one had asked for my side of the conversation. Newton had made me sound like a raging bitch when all I'd done was ask him a few direct questions that he was unable to answer.

I spoke with Bret Brzyscz, a former union rep and one of my field training officers, who thought the department had violated state law by placing that memo in my file without telling me about it or letting me read it ahead of time. My own research revealed that Bret was correct; California's Peace Officer Bill of Rights states, "No public safety officer shall have any comment adverse to his interest entered in his personnel file...without the public safety officer having first read and signed the instrument containing the adverse comment."

So why had they slipped this document in there? This was more than a clerical error. To me, this felt like a deliberate cover-up. In fact, when my lawyer notified the police department that I had not been aware of this memo in my file, the memo was later removed.

But what were they trying to hide?

I have a theory.

At some point in the lead-up to my written reprimand hearing, Hahn had allowed this bias and saw that his supervisors, from Bergstrom up to Moore, had botched their IA investigation. They hadn't investigated the allegations thoroughly, and they hadn't proved any wrongdoing. But in the process, they had violated my rights and discriminated against me. Not only had they violated my rights, but they had documented the discrimination with their IA reports and reprimand recommendations.

What's worse—I noticed.

When I met with Hahn about the written reprimand, I had pointed out in detail how the department had violated its own policy against discriminatory harassment.

"My marital status is the reason my work environment has become hostile," I wrote in my rebuttal.

Supervisors have passed judgment on me because it was said

that I was married with young children. Had the proper questions been asked in my interview, I don't believe my work environment would be hostile because the supervisors that have passed judgment would know the entire story, including my side and not just the side of an angry citizen who wrote a letter full of false allegations.

I think Hahn saw trouble coming. And I think he realized he needed to do two things. The first thing was he had to get rid of me while I was still on probation and had no legal recourse. The second thing he had to do was quash Walstad's and Moore's unfounded and seemingly discriminatory investigation and allegations, the one that Walstad said Hahn himself told him we would receive written reprimands for. By using the Newton phone call as his primary reason for terminating me, he was not obligated to investigate further. I was a probationary officer. He could let go of me whenever he wanted without having to provide a reason, as he affirmed in his deposition:

> Lawyer [to Hahn]: Did you request that anybody go interview Janelle and maybe an investigation be done to get her side of the story regarding this conversation with Sergeant Newton?
>
> Hahn: No.
>
> Lawyer: Why not?

Hahn: Because there was no need. I was releasing her from probation.

Lawyer: So you decided right then and there you were going to release her. You didn't care what she had to say about it?

Hahn: [...] This was basically the last straw. There were all these red flags leading up to this, and now she has a problem with a supervisor and is referring to her old agency how they do things. And then, thinking back to her background, how she had conflicts somewhat similar in her background, I just decided this wasn't a good fit for our department.

Lawyer: You didn't want to get her side of the story as to, you know, maybe her point of view as to what her take on the conversation with Sergeant Newton was?

Hahn: If this was the only thing that happened, I'm sure I would have, but there was a multitude of things.

Hahn's idea of "a multitude of things" included his belief that I wasn't getting along with other female officers. He said he'd heard this from Lieutenant Richardson, but he couldn't remember when they had the conversation, where they'd talked, or how the topic came up in the first place.

All of this sounded crazy to me. I liked Lieutenant Richardson and always got along well with her. What's more, out of around 127 sworn officers in Roseville at the time, I believe only around six were females. It's true that I was quiet and kept to myself, but I'd always had pleasant, professional relations with the other females in the office. There was no conflict, no tension. We weren't best friends, but I respected them and got along with them.

> Lawyer: How did it come back that you were talking to Lieutenant Richardson regarding Officer Perez?
>
> Hahn: I don't remember.
>
> Lawyer: Do you remember where the conversation took place?
>
> Hahn: I am assuming in the police station somewhere, but other than that, I don't.
>
> Lawyer: More specifically, like, do you recall was it in an office?
>
> Hahn: No.
>
> Lawyer: Do you remember what she told you?
>
> Hahn: Yeah. That female officers in the department had approached her and said, what's wrong with Janelle? She doesn't talk to us, or she's not friendly, or something along those lines.

Lawyer: Which female officers?

Hahn: I don't know.

Lawyer: How many female officers?

Hahn: I don't know.

Lawyer: How many female officers did you have working at the Roseville Police Department in August of 2012?

Hahn: I don't know. I assume it's around five or six.

I find this part of Hahn's deposition incredibly confusing. How can the chief of police be unable to recall a conversation—one of the factors he took into account for my termination—with a lieutenant over allegations that I didn't get along with other female officers?

Hahn latched onto a passing comment from Richardson because I believe he needed a smoking gun. I never had a single issue with another female officer in Roseville. In fact, I don't recall ever working with another female, with the exception of Richardson, who had, at some points, been my supervising lieutenant. But during my background check for the job, they had learned about some conflicts in South San Francisco—conflicts brought on not by me but by other female officers who were harassing me. I wasn't the problem. In fact, one reason they'd hired me in Roseville was because their background investigation found that I'd stayed above petty conflicts in my last job.

Lawyer: Do you remember in particular with Ms. Perez, does anything stick out in your mind as to why you hired her?

Hahn: Yeah. She had a very good background. Well, with all things considered, she had a very good background. Most of the comments were [that Janelle was] very proactive, hard-working. Those kinds of comments seem pretty typical if I remember correctly. There was something else about conflicts with some officers. Pretty much everybody said it was the other officers' fault, really. They didn't remember what it was about, but they believed it was initiated or spurred by other officers. Yet everybody said she was a really hard worker. I think it's pretty unanimous, everybody saying she was a hard worker.

Lawyer: So you have issues with female officers in South San Francisco. Lieutenant Richardson tells you that some unknown number and unknown identity female officers have a problem with Janelle?

Hahn: Hold on. [Richardson] didn't tell me it was unknown. I'm sure she knows who it was.

Lawyer: Didn't you want to know?

Hahn: No. I mean, I don't remember her telling me who it was. But you could ask her. She would know.

Lawyer: Do you remember what their specific complaint was?

Hahn: No. But you could ask her. She would know.

Lawyer: So generally describe for me, again, what Lieutenant Richardson told you the other officers' problem was.

Hahn: That multiple female officers had approached Lieutenant Richardson saying some sort of [Perez was] "hard to get along with," doesn't say "hello," something. I don't remember. Some sort of conflict.

Lawyer: You don't remember what, if anything, you said back to Lieutenant Richardson?

Hahn: No.

Lawyer: Did you hear anything more about this conflict with female officers?

Hahn: From Lieutenant Richardson?

Lawyer: Or anybody.

Hahn: No.

Did I keep to myself? Yes, I did. I was on probation. I was quiet. I did my work, and I worked hard.

Did I have problems with female officers? No. Did I like Sergeant Morris? Not particularly. I'd greet her when we passed in the hallway, but she never replied. She wasn't friendly. She always acted like she was above me, and I never felt comfortable with her. But I still said hello to her and never talked about her behind her back.

As far as the complaint against me in the domestic violence case, I never heard about it. To be perfectly honest, I don't even believe it ever existed—I never saw or heard anything related to this. Whoever took this particular complaint must not have thought it was important because no one ever investigated it, and no one ever asked me about it. In Hahn's deposition, he talks in circles about the importance of the complaint. It wasn't important enough to warrant an IA investigation, but it was apparently important enough to get me fired—without an investigation.

> Lawyer: Did that electronic complaint, did it come to you directly, or did it come to someone else?
>
> Hahn: Those go directly to the internal affairs office. Lieutenant Bergstrom is the one that told me about that.
>
> Lawyer: Why was it that Lieutenant Bergstrom came to you

to advise you that this electronic complaint had come in? Do you know?

Hahn: I don't know.

Lawyer: Would he have to come to you and advise you of every electronic complaint that came in at that time?

Hahn: Well, for sure if it was going to—he thought it was going to be a formal investigation, absolutely, because I have to authorize that.

Lawyer: Did it ever rise to a formal investigation?

Hahn: No.

Lawyer: Did anyone ever talk to Ms. Perez about this incident?

Hahn: I don't know.

Lawyer: Were you interested in hearing Ms. Perez's side of the story regarding this incident?

Hahn: Well, we would have if it was an internal affairs complaint, but it never became one, so—

Lawyer: But it's one of the factors something you took into account to—

Hahn: Correct.

Lawyer: —terminate her employment, right?

Hahn: To terminate her probation, yes.

Lawyer: Effectively terminate her employment, right?

Hahn: Yes.

Lawyer: You didn't care what her side of the story was?

Hahn: I didn't feel a need to get her side of the story at the time, no.

Lawyer: Why not?

Hahn: Because it wasn't an internal affairs complaint.

Does that sound like due process?

One thing that was nagging me about Hahn was this: Why did he hear my appeal of Moore's written reprimand if he had already decided to terminate me? If he wasn't going to ask for my side of the story about the coworkers and the domestic violence complaint, why bother to let me defend myself against Bergstrom, Walstad, and Moore's equally ridiculous charges? My lawyer asked about this during the lawsuit.

Lawyer: Why were you interested to see what she had to say about her letter of reprimand if you were going to terminate her anyway?

Hahn: Because she had a right to have an administrative hearing regarding discipline that she had gotten from this specific IA case. And I'm not about violating people's rights.

My lawyer seemed just as unconvinced of that last statement as I was. He pressed on, trying to pin down exactly when Hahn had made his decision to terminate me.

Lawyer: This written reprimand that Captain Moore gave to Officer Perez that you had scheduled to meet with her on and have her hearing on September 4, 2012, was this a factor that you took into account in your decision to terminate Ms. Perez?

Hahn: The facts contained in the internal affairs investigation were a factor in my decision to release her from probation, yes.

Lawyer: Which facts?

Hahn: The facts that she violated our cell phone policy.

Lawyer: But the letter of reprimand doesn't accuse her of violating the cell phone policy?

At this point in the deposition, Hahn's lawyer conveniently interjects. Perhaps his lawyer remembered how, just moments ago, Hahn stated that he'd decided *not* to release me from probation for "talking on the phone."

With Hahn constantly contradicting himself, it became impossible to know why he decided to terminate me. It was only after I was fired that the Roseville Police Department retroactively issued the charge Hahn said I'd been fired for.

A NEW CHARGE

There was one more clue that Hahn was seemingly trying to whitewash the flawed IA investigation to remove any suggestion that I'd been discriminated against. He did this by revising my written reprimand *after I'd been terminated*.

After my appeal hearing, Hahn sent my written reprimand back to Moore for amendments. Weeks after my termination, Glynn called me at home and said he would like to meet me to give me a copy of this new reprimand.

I was confused. I didn't work at the Roseville Police Department anymore. Why bother reprimanding me? Reprimands are designed to correct unwanted behaviors, and since I wouldn't be around to correct any behavior, what was the point?

I asked him to just mail it, but Glynn insisted on meeting in person. In his deposition, Glynn attested that he needed my signature on the document to confirm receipt. Of course, anyone can send a document by certified mail and get a signature to confirm the recipient got it. Why would it matter that I met Glynn in person?

I learned during the court case that this revised reprimand, issued after I was fired, was put in my file. The Peace Officer's Bill of Rights states that nothing can be put in an officer's file without their knowledge. It seems to me, the superiors in the department needed my signature so they could put this document in my file to cover the tracks of their inconsistent decision-making.

I met with Glynn and the president of the police association at a McDonald's in Roseville. Glynn handed me a memo from Captain Moore dated September 10, nearly a week after I'd been fired. In this version, the two original charges for unsatisfactory work performance and conduct unbecoming an officer were tagged "not sustained" and were superseded by a new reprimand for "extended or frequent use" of a personal phone. I also found a little humor in the situation—the memo dated September 10 said "to: Ofc Perez," yet I was NOT a police officer anymore. If I misrepresented this in the real world, I could be arrested for that; yet they still wrote "officer" on a document when I was actually no longer a police officer.

In the new version, Moore had removed his moralistic comments about my marital status and focused primarily on the phone calls I had with Shad during those five days in May. Clearly, Moore was stepping back and trying to remove any suggestion that I was being punished based on my marital status.

Was this something Hahn had ordered Moore to do to eliminate evidence that I was discriminated against? Hahn had a different excuse in the deposition:

Lawyer [to Hahn]: Did you tell him [Captain Moore] to go back and change the letter of reprimand?

Hahn: Yes.

Lawyer: Now, did it matter to you that you had already terminated Ms. Perez, she was no longer an employee of your department? So why go back and amend a letter of reprimand for an employee who had already been terminated?

Hahn: Because her right is to have an admin hearing...she has a right to get the results of that admin hearing regardless of whether she's an employee or not, and, again, I don't violate people's rights, so we followed policy.

It's hard to follow Hahn's logic here. He allowed me to defend myself against charges that he later claimed weren't grounds for termination. The result of that defense was that the original charges were not sustained. But then, here comes this brand-new third charge, for which there was no investigation and no opportunity for me to refute. Since this was a new charge, and since Hahn is all about following proper procedures and ensuring individual rights, why wasn't I given a chance to defend myself against this new charge?

I assume Hahn was trying to cover his ass. If I were to file a discrimination lawsuit against the department, he would need something—even an unsubstantiated claim—to justify terminating my probation. And that justification couldn't even hint that the department disapproved of my private relationships because that would be discriminatory.

To me, it was also significant that Newton's memo about our shift-trade conversation had no date on it. Newton later claimed that he wrote the memo the very same day we spoke. But memos in that department were all written from the same template, which automatically dated everything, so I think Newton had to have purposely deleted the date. This fueled my suspicion that the memo was written after I'd been fired and had been added to my file the same way my revised reprimand had been amended and sanitized after I'd been fired. The memo was just part of the seemingly phony record that the department created to hide the discriminatory way I was treated.

This new reprimand was just as flimsy as Hahn's other claims. The department had no idea whether the calls Shad and I made on those five days in May were more extended or more frequent than anyone else's in the department. Apparently, having an average of fifteen minutes of personal phone calls during an eleven-hour shift is in violation of their cell phone policy, regardless of the fact that officers can take multiple breaks throughout their shift. To know whether our phone use was excessive, you'd have to know how much time other officers spent using their personal phones. No one bothered to look at that, however. For all we know—and for all Bergstrom knew—the time I spent on the phone with Shad during those five days could have been a tiny fraction of the time other officers spent on their personal phones. The excessive phone use claim was just a red herring.

SHAD'S SPECIAL TREATMENT

Naturally, all this had a damaging effect on my relationship with Shad. As I said before, I was angry, and I resented that Shad was able to keep his job when I'd lost mine.

When the IA investigation concluded, Shad got off with just a written reprimand. While I kept my head down and tried to navigate the various written and unwritten policies of the department, Shad appeared to let loose. When Shad learned of the violations being brought forward in the IA investigation, he testified that he went into Bergstrom's office and yelled at him.

> Lawyer: This heated argument, I mean, you raised your voice with Lieutenant Bergstrom, right?
>
> Begley: Yes.
>
> Lawyer: And did he raise his voice with you?
>
> Begley: Yeah, he yelled at me.

I thought for sure Shad would get in trouble for this type of behavior. I know I would have been fired on the spot for yelling at Bergstrom the way Shad did. By the end of his shouting match with Bergstrom, Shad announced he was quitting the SWAT team. Shad also cornered Newton and complained about the investigation. Shad's behavior ensured everyone knew how he felt about the proceedings. But when my lawyer asked Bergstrom about this argument, Bergstrom wrote it off.

> Bergstrom: Shad came to me and said that he was going to resign from the SWAT team. And Shad's always been a very good member of the SWAT team. So I asked him why. He gave me an answer that I knew—I mean, I know him pretty well. I knew when he started talking to me that he wasn't telling me the whole truth. And so I just told him, "Look, if you've got

something you want to say, Shad, say it. If you have something that you are upset about, then let's not sit here and beat around the bush. Tell me." And he did. You know, there was a lot of emotion from him, and I understand that. And as it was, I had some other issues of why he was leaving the SWAT team. Those repaired themselves and he ended up coming back, probably, I want to say [...] it was six months to a year later, and we ended up adding him back on the SWAT team.

Lawyer: Was part of his being upset related to the investigation of him and Officer Perez?

Bergstrom: That was why he was upset. [...] He was upset about the entire process. He was upset at me for being involved in the process. He was just mad, and I was the brunt of some of that, you know.

Lawyer: Did he face any disciplinary actions for having a heated exchange with you?

Bergstrom: No.

But Shad and Bergstrom were buddies—they were both on the SWAT team—so I guess that kind of behavior was accepted between male colleagues.

Lawyer: Did they do another investigation against you for this heated argument you had with Lieutenant Bergstrom?

Begley: No.

Lawyer: Nothing came of that, right?

Begley: No.

Lawyer: When describing the Roseville Police Department, did you ever come to the conclusion that it was like an old boys' club, or have you ever used that term, old boys' club?

Begley: Good ol' boys?

Lawyer: Good ol' boys. Something like that.

Begley: Yeah, I think that there was—I was under the opinion that there was a little bit of that going on.

When Shad yelled at Bergstrom, he was treated like one of the good ol' boys. But after I asked questions about a shift trade, without ever raising my voice, I was fired.

I was close with my dad throughout the investigation and the aftermath. My dad stayed by my side through it all, and I valued and respected his advice. After I lost my job, he became insistent. "You need to stop seeing Shad," my dad urged. "He's not good for you." I realized he was right. Shad and I stopped seeing each other in November.

Through all this, what stuck with me was the unfairness of it all. I'd been fired, and Shad, who had done the same thing I had, kept his job. But, as Hahn pointed out several times, the chief didn't need a reason to let a probationary officer go. He could do it without cause at any time, and the officer had no right to appeal.

But an officer who was wrongfully terminated—based on discrimination—could sue.

CHAPTER 5

FILING THE LAWSUIT

I contacted a lawyer shortly after Hahn told me that I was being terminated for "failing to complete probation successfully." At first, I had no intention of filing a lawsuit. I just wanted to get my job back, and I felt having an attorney do that for me would send the signal that I was serious. I thought I'd have a better chance of being reinstated.

Sometime later, I was talking with Bret, my former field training officer. Bret disagreed with how I had been treated. He mentioned the name of the lawyer who had sued the city in the gay discrimination case. His name was Paul Goyette. I decided to give Goyette a phone call.

Goyette got right to the point.

"This is bullshit," he said after I explained the circumstances. "You got screwed. Anybody can see that."

At the same time, he said my case would be challenging because I had been a probationary officer. But he was willing to represent me.

"I should tell you that I am, in reality, not a very nice person," he admitted. "I'm a competitive asshole that pretty much only cares about achieving and winning."

That sounded good to me because I wanted someone who was going to be aggressive about standing up to Hahn, Moore, and some of these other sanctimonious supervisors in Roseville who felt they had a right to pass judgment on my personal life.

In early December 2012, Goyette spoke with the city's attorney and outlined our case. We just want to get her job back, he explained. The city's attorney said she would talk with Hahn and the city's human resources department and get back to us, but the city's attorney didn't sound like she would be easy to work with.

She wasn't. She called back and insisted there wasn't any gender bias. She told Goyette, "The male officer would have been terminated too had he been on probation." The attorney's response was significant because it indicated that the IA investigation would have been grounds for terminating Shad—which means that it was also the grounds for terminating me.

Remember, by that point, the department had pulled back the original charges and stacked up several other complaints as the "reasons" I was terminated: supposed violation of the cell phone policy, the vague domestic violence complaint, Newton's claim that I was agitated in requesting a shift trade, and the never-investigated allegations that I was not getting along with other female officers. If these were the real reasons I'd been fired, why would the city's attorney say Shad would have been fired, too? The city's attorney had seemingly put her foot in her mouth—and made it clear that I'd been fired over my relationship with Shad, not the other "reasons" the department had stated.

As my lawyer got deeper into settlement discussions with the city's attorney, Goyette asked me for a detailed bullet-point list of my reasons for my discrimination claims.

I wrote back the next day and didn't hold anything back.

THE CASE FOR GENDER DISCRIMINATION

The whole question of whether I was a malcontent or couldn't get along with the other females on the force was very troubling to me.

For one thing, I'm naturally quiet. I'm not a particularly outgoing person. I'm more of an introvert.

At work, I kept to myself. I was new, and I was on probation, and I was always careful not to call attention to myself the way some people love to do. I just wanted to do my job well and then go home every night.

But some days, it was more difficult than others. One day the supervisor I was working under at the time, Sergeant Slate, told me that I needed to start boxing during my workouts. "A woman needs to know how to box," he said.

But I didn't feel the need to hit a coworker in the face or be hit in the face by a coworker, so I continued to do my regular workouts. Slate hounded me about it.

After I switched to swing shift, my new supervisor, Sergeant Frank Kander, called me into his office. He was working on my evaluation, and he asked whether I'd had any issues with Slate. I told him no.

Kander said Slate had just sent him an email claiming that I wasn't a good team member. I didn't help my fellow team members and refused to stay late to complete my work. But Kander said he'd consulted with my current team members, and they'd all commented on how helpful I was. I was a great team player, Kander said.

"I've asked all the guys on my team about you," he said. "They all say you're super helpful. If they need anything, you're always there. So I don't know where Slate is coming from. Did he ever sit down and talk to you about his concerns?"

"No," I said. "This is the first I've heard of it."

I asked to see Slate's email, but Kander said he couldn't share it with me.

"I'm not going to write any of his comments in your evaluation because A, he didn't talk to you about them and B, I've talked to your team members, and everyone said you're a great team player."

I appreciated that, but I was still troubled that Slate had, in my eyes, unfairly criticized me. I believed Slate was unhappy I didn't box with him, and from what I heard from others at the department, I believed Slate felt that women did not belong in law enforcement.

"I'd like to take this to the lieutenant," I said. "I believe Sergeant Slate has an alleged history of discrimination against women, and to me, that's what this is about."

"Listen," Kander said. "You're on probation. Don't stir the pot. I'm not going to put anything into your evaluation that he said that's negative because my guys are saying just the opposite. So don't worry about it."

But I did worry about it. I went to talk to Sam Bosch, who was on Slate's team and had worked with me when I was training on the same team. Bosch was widely acknowledged to be the laziest officer on staff. He never did more than the bare minimum. He never offered to help and was out the door a second after his shift ended. He didn't even sit in the same room with us.

"How was your evaluation from Slate?" I asked him.

"Great," Bosch said.

"Did he say anything to you about staying late and helping other officers?"

"No," Bosch said.

So Slate gives the laziest guy in the department a glowing review but goes out of his way to try and get negative comments into the evaluation of the new female officer. I was appalled.

WOMEN ON THE FORCE

I was not the only female officer who thought the Roseville Police Department discriminated against women. After we filed our lawsuit, we took the deposition of Mary Green, who was a detective in the department. She started out the deposition giving one-word answers, and I remember thinking that she was just trying to protect everyone. As she went on, I realized that she was probably afraid of saying something that would make things worse for her.

She talked about how she applied for a special assignment and didn't feel the selection process was fair and equitable. She had applied to be on the crime suppression unit. Instead of a panel interview, she was interviewed by Sergeant Slate behind a Chevron gas station on Pleasant Grove. She thought the informal meeting was "irregular." Later, Slate called her and asked if he could stop by her house.

He told her he had some bad news. She hadn't gotten the promotion because Slate had gone with "one of my guys."

> Lawyer: So what did you take "my guys" to mean?

> Green: I took it to mean that he had to go with his boys.

We asked if she had complained about her treatment. She hesitated, then admitted she had. Reluctantly.

> Green: I don't like to complain. I was nervous about how I would be perceived within the department for making a complaint. I wasn't sure if I was off base on my feelings about the selection process, and I didn't know that I wanted to deal with everything around it.

Lawyer: In your mind, is there a perception of female officers who speak up rather than accepting, I guess, the sort of treatment that they're given?

Roseville Lawyer: Calls for speculation. Vague.

Green: Are you asking specifically in my department or within law enforcement in general?

Lawyer: Just your experience within the Roseville Police Department.

Green: That was one of my fears in coming forward.

Lawyer: I guess I'm just trying to figure out where that fear comes from...and I'm just curious as to why you felt afraid, based on your gender, going forward and making a complaint.

Green: Well, I think there's a negative association that comes forward with that, and you don't want to play into the stereotypes. And then additionally it's a supervisor. It's someone who is fairly well-regarded and well-respected without our department.

Lawyer: You were afraid that any complaint that you made toward Sergeant Slate being a SWAT member would likewise not be taken seriously?

Green: Correct.

So it seemed that guys like Slate had free reign to behave however they wanted to. In her deposition, Green mentioned one night she was working late and turned in a report to Slate. They started chatting and the topic turned to family. Green had a child at home. Slate asked Green if she'd ever consider staying at home with her child.

"That would be great," Green had said, "but we have two mortgages, and I can't do it."

Slate did not drop the subject. "You should let go of one of your mortgages and stay at home with your daughter," he told Green. "You need to think about what's important." Although Green testified under oath to this conversation, to my knowledge, Slate has not publicly admitted that it occurred.

"Did you take that statement to be motivated by gender discrimination?" my lawyer asked.

Green replied, "Yes."

Green eventually went to HR to file a complaint against Slate. The letter described the hostile work environment, asked for an investigation, and requested that the behavior be stopped. Although Green had purposely avoided going to someone in her direct chain of command, news about the complaint got out, and it eventually got back to Green that Captain Moore was upset with her about the letter.

We asked Green what she thought of Moore.

> Green: My professional opinion is that Captain Moore is very smart. However, he is ingrained in his ways and oftentimes unwilling to change.
>
> Lawyer: In what ways is he ingrained?
>
> Green: That once he forms an opinion that there is no changing it. That is what it's going to be. Sort of the "you think like me; you do what I think is right; therefore, you must be right."
>
> Lawyer: And so if you disagree with Captain Moore in your experience—
>
> Green: I generally did not disagree with Captain Moore.
>
> Lawyer: And what would the reason for that be?
>
> Green: Because I saw what happened to other people when they disagreed with him. You know what? I didn't see. I had heard.

I know I certainly found Green's last statement to be true.

When I refused to sign his written reprimand, I crossed him, and I believe I paid for it later. Refusing to sign the reprimand—even though it was within my rights to refuse to sign—spelled the end of my time on the police force in Roseville. I didn't realize it at the time because no one had warned me about Moore, and I didn't know the man well enough to understand that crossing him like that was a bad mistake. Simply put, I pissed off the wrong person by standing up for myself. My belief is Moore was not a supporter of women in law enforcement.

Then my lawyer asked Green if discrimination was part of the department's overarching problems. She acknowledged it was and went on to describe how, after giving birth to her daughter, Walstad had assigned her to ride with a field training officer on her first day back from light duty. None of the male officers were forced to do that when returning from light duty. In another incident, she called Walstad to tell him that her nanny was late arriving to her house and that Green would be late to shooting training at the rifle range. Walstad said that was fine. Green showed up around ten minutes late—and so did another male officer who was carrying a Starbucks cup. During her deposition, Green said a short while after she arrived late, Walstad informed Green that he was going to have to write her up for being late to the rifle range. The male officer did not receive a write-up.

To me, the way Walstad, Slate, and Morris acted reflected

an institutional way of thinking. Even Morris, who later described in her deposition several instances of gender bias against her, seemed insensitive to the institutional discrimination going on in Roseville. The attitudes were embedded in the culture there, and because there were so few women and so much fear, no one ever called the men out on their behavior.

"I JUST WANTED TO GET ALONG"

When we took Sergeant Morris' deposition, she also admitted she'd experienced gender discrimination in Roseville. She talked about the time when she was pregnant with her child, and she was demoted from being a sworn officer with a badge and a gun to a community services officer. Those jobs are mostly held by civilians who help with traffic control and clerical work. She said certain male officers didn't want to work with her, forced her to take positions in the rear when police were entering a building, or told her to go be a wife instead of a police officer. She said her male counterparts had a betting pool that she wouldn't pass the motor academy. People threatened to resign if she got promoted to sergeant.

Morris had been in Roseville for many years at that point, so she'd been around that kind of behavior a long time. She said the only time she filed a formal complaint was when a lieutenant called her stupid and incompetent in a briefing before a large group. During her deposition, Morris described how she asked for an IA investigation on the incident, but the captain told her the lieutenant was just an asshole, everyone knew it, and she should just get over it.

"I just wanted to get along, and I wanted to just be left alone," she said, explaining why she didn't pursue her complaint.

Hearing Morris and Green tell these stories helped me realize that at the Roseville Police Department, if you speak up and stand up for yourself, you can quickly become a target. And I was an easy target because I was on probation. I realized that the department needed someone to come in and turn it upside down. They needed leadership that wasn't going to tolerate discrimination. They needed people to stand up for themselves and lieutenants and sergeants who respect people who stand up for themselves. Someone like me. Someone like Bret. Instead, they fostered a department of bullies.

During my time at the Roseville Police Department, I recognized this discrimination for what it was. Several of my male superiors had an apparent history of discriminating against the few women in the department, but they held the power, and we didn't. Even so, I wasn't going to admit to charges that weren't true. I refused to be bullied, and I lost my job.

"SOME PEOPLE WERE NOT FANS OF WOMEN IN LAW ENFORCEMENT"

Bret was the officer who knew me best at Roseville. I trained under a number of field training officers, but I spent more time with Bret than anyone, and I was always comfortable with him. I wouldn't say we were close friends, but for the most part, I felt like I could trust him and that he had my best interests in mind. I really didn't trust anyone completely.

Bret had been on the force for about twelve years and had previously served on the Police Officer's Association. In that role, he often had to stand by officers when it came to disciplinary matters. It had been his job to ensure officers weren't steamrolled or treated unfairly by those in the command structure. I'm not saying he was antagonistic toward the department's leaders, but he also wasn't afraid to stand up to them when he saw that someone was being treated unfairly or was wrongly accused, or something. He seemed very sensitive to any sign of inequality. This hadn't done anything for his career, unfortunately; although he was one of the best police officers I had seen at the Roseville PD, he'd been passed over for promotions several times, and a lot of people chalked that up to how he held the department's leaders accountable.

While other officers were tight-lipped during depositions, Bret was more willing to speak up against disparities he saw in how the few women in our department were treated.

One of the first instances my lawyer asked Bret about was the book Sergeant Morris had told me to read—and me alone, out of all the other probationary police officers.

> Lawyer: Did any of those other trainees you had during this time period, were they asked to read the book on emotional survival by Sergeant Morris?
>
> Brzyscz: I don't know.
>
> Lawyer: Did any of those trainees comment to you that they were being told to read this book?
>
> Brzyscz: No. None of them told me they were required to read the book.
>
> Lawyer: Now, as part of your program, when you were serving as an FTO (field training officer), as part of your program of training your trainees, did you as an FTO ever require your trainees to read a book on emotional survival?
>
> Brzyscz: I did not. However, it was—my attention was brought that at the very least, Ms. Perez was told to read that book. But as far as dealing with the other trainees, I don't recall that ever coming up, nor was I required to read that book.
>
> Lawyer: Did it concern you when Ms. Perez told you that Sergeant Morris required her to read this book and report to her

during her off-duty hours? Did that concern you from a field training officer's point of view?

Brzyscz: Yes, it did.

Lawyer: Why?

Brzyscz: Well, because I think if you're required to do something, you should be compensated for it. So that was my main concern [...]

I don't know if the episode with Bret calling Morris and Richardson about the book led the two officers to conclude that I was a complainer or slacker. It may have. But the truth was that I read the book like I was told to, and when I was finished, I discussed the book with Morris, just as I'd been told to do. I didn't complain to Bret about reading it; I just told him that was what I had to do when I got off work.

Bret's deposition was particularly damaging to the police department for how clearly he was able to point out inconsistencies in the department's rules. As a field training officer, Bret was well-versed in all the various rules, regulations, and accepted practices of being a police officer for Roseville. And when we asked him about issues like dating a coworker, extramarital affairs, or using your personal cell phone while on duty, he said the rules, if they existed, were never enforced, with one notable exception: me.

Lawyer: Have you ever become aware of anyone who has been reprimanded, counseled, or disciplined because of their personal dating relationship with a coworker?

Brzyscz: No. Well, yeah, no.

Lawyer: Did you ever gain direct knowledge of or even hear rumors of other officers being involved in extramarital affairs?

Brzyscz: Yes.

Lawyer: Did you ever become aware of whether the department ever conducted any type of internal affairs investigation related to other officers' involvements in extramarital affairs?

Brzyscz: I have no knowledge of there being any sort of internal affairs investigation about any extramarital affairs.

Lawyer: Have you ever heard of a policy or even a practice where officers are required to, say, keep their supervisor advised when they get separated from a spouse?

Brzyscz: I have no knowledge of any policy or practice of that nature.

Lawyer: Typically, it's nobody's business?

Brzyscz: Yeah. I've never heard of that happening.

Lawyer: Does the department have any policy regarding limitations in terms of time, whether it be minutes or messages for an officer's personal use of his cell phone device while on duty that you are aware of?

Brzyscz: Not that I am aware of. And I would like to clarify an answer that I gave earlier about saying that I had no idea there's a policy in place about cell phone usage. I had heard after Ms. Perez was let go that there was some question about it being regarding to some sort of cell phone usage. So a better answer would be, I don't know what the policy is, and that would be the first time that I was aware of it.

Lawyer: What is your practice on the job? Do you carry both a personal cell phone and—

Brzyscz: I have my personal and then my work-related.

Lawyer: I would assume that throughout the course of your shift, you probably use your personal device periodically throughout the course of your shift?

Brzyscz: Yes.

Lawyer: And would that be fair for me to say both for telephone calls and possibly text messages?

Brzyscz: Yes.

Lawyer: Possibly even personal emails, maybe?

Brzyscz: Yes.

Lawyer: And just based on all your years of service at the Roseville Police Department, plus your service on the POA board, would it be fair for me to say that most officers operate under a similar process to what you do?

Brzyscz: Yes.

Lawyer: And are you aware of any officer ever being reprimanded, counseled, or disciplined for their use of their personal device while on duty?

Brzyscz: No.

Lawyer: While you were training Ms. Perez or any other trainee, did you ever counsel them as to what the do's and don'ts were about using their personal device while on duty?

Brzyscz: I don't recall that ever coming up.

Lawyer: When you got trained up and went through, I think you described it as a two-week program to be a trainer, did you get any information there that taught you to teach your trainees to be careful about their personal cell phone device use while on duty?

Brzyscz: No.

Bret went on to describe the protocol for taking breaks. Officers are allowed to take a break for lunch and to take breaks periodically throughout the day. When you tell the dispatcher that you are "code seven," that means you are on lunch.

Lawyer: When you're on a code seven, is it acceptable then to, say, call home and see what's going on?

Brzyscz: Yeah.

Lawyer: Is that a common practice?

Brzyscz: I would say it's common to be able to while you're working and you are not even at code seven to be able to call home and check in, yeah.

As I listened to Bret testify in his deposition, I couldn't help but think, *"What will a jury think when they hear this?"* Hahn testified that the IA was one of the factors in my termination. Yet even the field training officers knew of no restrictions and were never ordered to mention it to trainees. What's more, it was commonplace for officers during the course of their regular workday to occasionally make or take personal calls while on duty. Not only are trainees never alerted to these alleged rules about cell phones, but as they are working, they are watching all manner of police officers making and taking personal calls throughout the day. As a new officer, you have to conclude that this practice is no big deal. It's certainly not an offense any officer would expect to be fired over. Again, any officer but me, a woman who'd become a thorn in the department's side.

When asked about his opinion on my firing, Bret said he felt it was related to my gender and my relationship with Shad and not cell phone use as Hahn stated.

> Lawyer: Did it concern you that the department terminated Ms. Perez?
>
> Brzyscz: It did, it did concern me.
>
> Lawyer: Why?
>
> Brzyscz: Because for all practical reasons [...] there were no issues with her as an employee.
>
> Lawyer: Did you have concerns that the department's termination of Ms. Perez may have been the result of her dating relationship with Officer Begley?
>
> Brzyscz: Yes.
>
> Lawyer: What caused you to think that or have those concerns?

Brzyscz: [...] Based on everything I saw and was aware of, I didn't see there being another reason for termination.

Lawyer: Did you have any concerns that the department may have terminated Ms. Perez because she's a woman?

Brzyscz: That did concern me.

Lawyer: Why is that? Well, I will ask it this way: There have been other incidents regarding women in the Roseville Police Department that have served as a foundation for your concern regarding Ms. Perez, right?

Brzyscz: That's correct.

Bret went on to explain that Mary Green had consulted with him at least twice about concerns that she was being treated differently than other members of the department. Green had not been selected for a crime suppression unit because Sergeant Slate decided to go with "one of his guys." He also described a time Green was written up for mishandling evidence, even though it wasn't entirely her fault.

Lawyer: In the well over a decade that you have been at the Roseville Police Department, did you ever get the impression besides the conclusions or the specific information you got regarding Mary Green or the conclusions you came to regarding Janelle Perez and her case, did you ever get the conclusion that the department had a culture, if you will, that was not friendly, receptive, encouraging, or supportive for women as police officers?

Roseville Lawyer: Calls for speculation. Lacks foundation. Go ahead.

Brzyscz: I wouldn't say that the entirety of the department necessarily had that. But I would say that [...] it seemed like there were some people who were not fans of women in law enforcement. But as far as—I just want to be clear. I don't think it's, like, everyone at the department has this opinion, that seems to be either a handful of people [...], but some people, I wouldn't say all.

Lawyer: Understood. That makes sense. But when you say a handful of people or a group of people, can you identify any specific people that fall into that group or category? Or let me ask it this way, not to put you on the spot too badly: Were any of those people that you are thinking of right now, were they in a decision-making role with Ms. Perez's case?

Brzyscz: I believe—

Roseville Lawyer: Calls for speculation. Go ahead.

Brzyscz: I believe they were.

Lawyer: So now I do have to ask: Who? Would Captain Moore be one of those people?

Brzyscz: I believe Captain Moore would have been one of those people.

That group, Bret thought, also included Slate, Moore, and another officer, but did not include Walstad or Newton.

Listening to this, it struck me once again that when I refused to sign Moore's reprimand that I had sealed my own fate. I had pissed off the wrong person. In Moore's eyes, it was bad enough that I was a woman. But to be a woman who stands up for herself and refused to shrink from what felt like his intimidation is probably too much for his fragile manhood to bear. I was toast the second I stood up to him.

Lawyer: Do you think the mere fact that Officer Perez confronted Captain Moore on this [her reprimand] and refused to sign the document had anything to do with her termination?

Brzyscz: The circumstances that you are talking about are cause for concern for me when she was terminated.

Lawyer: What do you mean?

Brzyscz: Well, I mean, technically, a letter of instruction is a one-year letter. It's not considered discipline, and no one is obligated to sign it. So if you're my boss and I did something wrong and you give me a letter of instruction, and I say, I am not going to sign it, and you say, "Okay, it's going to go in your file." The only obligation is that you let someone know it's going in the file. If they refuse to sign it, that's totally within their right to do so. So you know, based on the conversations I had with Shad Begley and Janelle Perez and the facts and circumstances that I knew about the case, that did concern me, because it went from a letter of instruction to termination, and I don't—obviously I don't know any of the pieces in between, but yeah, that concerned me.

Lawyer: Well, telling Captain Moore "no" generally is not good for one's career necessarily, right?

Roseville Lawyer: Objection. Argumentative. Calls for speculation.

Brzyscz: I would say that during that time period that this was going on, that that is an accurate statement.

Bret testified that in the twelve years he'd been on the Roseville Police Department, there had only been around ten female police officers. That's not ten in one year—that's ten women total who'd ever worked in the Roseville Police Department in over a decade.

INCONSISTENT ACCOUNTABILITY

In relaying the gender discrimination I'd faced at the department, I told my lawyer about my experience on the graveyard shift, the last team I'd worked with in Roseville. The men on this team had never made me feel welcome or comfortable. They helped *each other* out, but consistently ignored me if I needed any help.

They often made disparaging comments about women. One officer, also a probationary officer at the time, mentioned how a female police officer had married a male police officer and soon after had left her job. "Thank God," the officer concluded, suggesting that he felt women had no place in police work. On another occasion, on a stolen vehicle stop near Thunder Valley, an officer found a folding knife in a woman suspect's purse. "Not to sound sexist, but what's a chick doing with this kind of knife?" the officer said. By then, I'd come across enough of these comments that I'd started jotting some of these things down on my phone in case I needed them later.

I also filled my lawyer in about Andrew Knapp, the married probationary police officer who had worked with Shad. I thought Knapp was the perfect example of gender discrimination at play in Roseville. Although I had been working there when Knapp worked there too, I did not work with him or know him at all. Shad filled me in with all the details that he knew about Knapp. Knapp had worked in San Jose, and his wife was still living in the Bay Area when Knapp started in Roseville. Despite his marital status, Knapp frequently met his girlfriend at the police station to have lunch. No one launched an IA investigation into this juicy little arrangement. To my knowledge, no one issued reprimands to Knapp, claiming he was "unprofessional" and bringing shame and embarrassment to the Roseville police force.

Now, a lot of people talk at the police department, and I had heard that Knapp was the subject of an IA investigation while on probation. I heard that it had something to do with hitting on a woman at a gas station while working; I can't be certain of the reason. I do know that Knapp was not fired as a result of this IA investigation.

There were clear differences between how Knapp and I had each been treated while on probation. During Hahn's deposition in my case, he defended his decision to fire me by describing to my lawyer how he typically handled people on probation.

> Hahn: As a general rule in law enforcement, if somebody is on probation and is getting ready to get disciplined, you don't give them discipline. You release them from probation because if they've done something egregious enough to get disciplined in that period of time when they are supposed to be on their best behavior, it is not a good idea. You release them.

So, where was this same ethic when it came to Knapp? Knapp was never released from probation, despite alleged blatant public behavior that was far worse than mine.

Hahn's logic about minding your "P's and Q's" during probation couldn't fly here. There was one main difference: Knapp was male.

In 2012, an officer named Thomas Cabral allegedly made advances on a married woman while on duty and in uniform. The woman filed a complaint against Cabral and later filed a lawsuit against the City of Roseville on the grounds that Cabral had allegedly stalked her.

Her complaint triggered an IA investigation into Cabral's behavior, but before the investigation was finished, Cabral resigned from the department, possibly at the encouragement of his superiors. It sure was nice that Cabral had the opportunity to resign and not be fired—because he could then go on to apply to a new department with a clear record. The lawsuit was settled out of court, and the IA investigation was closed before it was concluded because Cabral no longer worked at the department.[3] Therefore, the allegations against Cabral were never admitted or proven.

---

3 "Former Roseville Officer Accused of Stalking Woman," *ABCNews 10*, September 18, 2013.

Compare that with the revised IA findings and the Newton memo that were placed in my file after I'd been terminated. Now remember, according to Hahn, he's not about violating people's rights—which was his reason for *continuing* an investigation *after* I was terminated. The allegations against Cabral, if true, are much more egregious than me having an off-duty relationship with a coworker. Our two experiences happened within months of each other. After my experience, I concluded the scarlet letter only gets assigned to female police officers. How else could Cabral have gotten out of his landslide of allegations scot-free?

After my termination, it was clear I wouldn't receive justice from the Roseville Police Department. I would have to ask the courts to validate my claim. It was time to sue the city.

WHAT WE SUED FOR

At this point, remember, all I wanted was to get my job back. My lawyer thought that was unlikely to happen.

"They'll throw money at you all day long before they give you your job back," he said.

Ultimately, Hahn rejected our proposal to resolve the case through a confidential mediator, so in October 2013, I decided to move ahead with a lawsuit against the department.

The accusations in the federal complaint that we filed against the City of Roseville included:

- Sex discrimination—Title VII of the Civil Rights Act of 1964
- Sex discrimination—California Fair Employment and Housing Act
- Violation of Civil Rights under the First, Fourth, and Fourteenth Amendment of the United States Constitution
- Due Process Violation under the Fourteenth Amendment of the United States Constitution
- Due Process Violation under the California State Constitution—State Claim
- Wrongful Termination in Violation of Public Policy

We felt there were strong precedents to support our claim that officers and employees of police departments have a right to privacy in private, off-duty sexual behavior.

One of the precedents we cited was a case in El Segundo, California, where a female clerk-typist in the city's police department applied to become a police officer. During a pre-employment polygraph test, the applicant said she'd once had a miscarriage and that the father had been a married officer in the department. She asked that the information be kept confidential, but it was shared with department personnel who were considering her application, and she was ultimately not hired. She sued.

The court ruled in that case that it was a violation of the woman's constitutional right to privacy to be refused employment because of her sexual activities when there was no evidence it would affect her job performance.

Would the court see the same kind of discrimination at play in my case? I was confident the judges would see the disparity and discrimination I saw. My confidence held, until it became jaded by my experience in the courts.

CHAPTER 6

GETTING MY STORY HEARD

In the fall of 2014, we began preparing for our upcoming depositions. I was concerned about what I perceived as my attorneys' lack of aggressiveness. My first attorney, a capable and organized associate named Marion, had left Goyette's firm and had been replaced by Sean O'Dowd, a young, fresh-faced lawyer who looked like a recent graduate. I wasn't sure he was tough enough to go up against the city's lawyers.

My father wanted to hire a public relations firm to publicize my case. My lawyer advised against that, and so we held off. But my father did write a letter to the mayor and city council about my lawsuit.

In it, he described the Roseville Police Department as "one

of the last bastions of male dominance" and a "good old boys club." The department was rife with bias, including Hahn, my father thought.

"Just because [Hahn] is black doesn't mean he is without prejudice, and to many within the department, he is an avowed sexist," my father wrote. "It is my belief that Captain Stefan Moore, Lieutenant Troy Bergstrom, Lieutenant Cal Walstad, Lieutenant Marc Glynn, and (untouchable) Kelby Newton all were involved. It seems as though they are all afraid of him. We are pursuing this as a civil matter, and I hope for the sake of your city that none of them fabricated evidence or were involved in a conspiracy to cover this up by destroying evidence of any type."

My dad didn't pull any punches when talking about Hahn. He thought the department was sexist and discriminatory. He told how he felt Hahn was "rude, condescending, and bullying" to me and said it was his goal to get the federal government to intervene and "straighten this department out." He mentioned a wrongful termination case against the US Postal Service in which a former employee fought in the courts for twelve years but finally got his job back with back pay. He also subtly reminded the city about the case in 2010 when employees sued over the department's anti-gay culture.

"I will do everything within my power to get this command

staff thrown out and hopefully replace it with a female police chief. My daughter aspired to be a leader within the department, and she gets terminated while her counterpart never missed a day of work. Sounds fundamentally flawed to me, and I hope to all of you who are reasonable people."

My father was trying to get them to sit down with us. See reason. Listen to our side. And reinstate a good cop to a job she enjoyed and performed with skill and strong intent.

No one from Roseville ever responded to the letter.

I'm not sure how my attorney felt about the letter, but I do know that Goyette was adamantly opposed to trying to generate publicity for my story. My dad was just as adamant that we needed to get the media involved so we could apply pressure to the city and get them to put me back on the job. Ultimately, I listened to Goyette, but that decision remains one of my biggest mistakes. This is where I allowed myself to respect the process, ultimately learning the hard way that it didn't respect me in return. I felt some stories detailing how the Roseville Police Department discriminated against women would gain a lot of attention and give us some leverage in my case.

For the next several months, the city just sat on its hands. I refused to meet with them to settle the case unless they would agree to consider giving me my job back. I would not change my stance on that. My attorneys were always after me to just sit down and listen to what the city might offer, but I refused. The city was just as adamant, so we were in a standoff.

"As of today, with the way I feel about this case, they could offer me a million dollars and not include my job, and I would not take that settlement," I told my attorney after the city had contacted us to discuss a settlement. "If you need to tell them that to get the point across to all of them that I am serious, then please do."

THE WORD GETS OUT

Despite Goyette's resistance to publicizing the case, the media nevertheless caught wind of it. Numerous TV stations aired stories on my case, and *The Sacramento Bee* reported on my lawsuit. *The Bee* pointed out that although both Shad and I were reprimanded, I was the only one who was fired.

Shad not only got to keep his job, but I believe he got favorable treatment from the department after I was fired. Although he had quit the SWAT team during the IA investigation, he rejoined SWAT shortly after my termination. He was then quickly given a special assignment as a school resource officer. By that time, the Roseville Police Department was well aware that I was working with a lawyer.

When I look back on it now, Shad was not only treated much better than I was; he may have been given preferential treatment. I believe Hahn, Moore, and the command staff wanted Shad to feel an obligation to them, so Shad wouldn't make a bigger stink about the unfair way I was treated. And I think Shad obliged them. I think he went into self-protection mode.

You could see this when we took Shad's deposition. He was vague in many of his responses, and like most of the officers who'd given depositions, he wasn't particularly forthcoming. There were a lot of short "yes" and "no" answers and a lot of "gosh, I can't remember" answers. For instance, when we asked him if he left the Roseville Police Department in 2014 because of how he was treated during the IA investigation, he denied that had anything to do with it. "I was just ready to work somewhere else," he said.

Newton talked about Shad's transfer differently. During Newton's deposition, my lawyer asked whether Shad had talked to Newton about his reasons for leaving, and Newton said Shad was "mad about how the IA was done and handled."

It's true that Shad backed me up on all the key points I'd made. He denied having sexual encounters with me on the job. He admitted being angry about the investigation. He admitted that some officers blatantly ignored certain regulations, such as the one against using tobacco on the job or in private. He admitted that officers routinely used their personal cell phones while on duty and he agreed that at least one member of the department had a bias against women. He said he'd heard about certain officers who were into the swinger lifestyle. He talked a little about his loud argument with Bergstrom and admitted that he felt Bergstrom had lied to him about aspects of that investigation.

Lawyer: Well, you disagreed with the department's decision, of course, to terminate Janelle, right?

Begley: Yes.

Lawyer: And, really why they gave you a letter of reprimand was somehow they viewed your relationship with Janelle Perez as somehow, some way inappropriate, right?

Begley: I don't feel like I got reprimanded for violating policy. I got reprimanded for violating the moral, I guess, compass of a lieutenant or captain. So, yeah, I think it was based on their opinions of an inappropriate relationship, not on department policy.

Lawyer: Now, when you say this somehow violated the moral compass of a lieutenant or captain, who are you referring to?

Begley: Lieutenant Walstad.

Lawyer: Anyone else?

Begley: I guess not so much. [...] What sticks out in my mind is what Lieutenant Walstad wrote. That's where the compass is based from, so I don't know if Captain Moore said anything or wrote anything to the same extent as Lieutenant Walstad. But Lieutenant Walstad, you can read in his findings that he was—I guess he didn't agree with our relationship.

My lawyer then focused in again on Shad's rebuttal.

Lawyer: When you write in the last sentence there [referring to Shad's written rebuttal]. "When Captain Moore gave me the reprimand, I asked him how much of the reprimand had to do with the terms 'a married coworker.' And he told me it had a lot to do with it." Do you remember Captain Moore telling you that?

Begley: Yes.

Lawyer: Did you come to the conclusion that the reason they were giving you a written reprimand is because you were involved in a relationship with Janelle, and they viewed Janelle as being married?

Begley: I think that my opinion is they were considering us both to be married, and we were having an extramarital affair, and that's more a reason that we got reprimanded than any policies being violated.

Lawyer: Did you form any opinion as to why the department terminated Janelle?

Begley: My opinion is that Janelle got terminated because of our relationship.

Shad is being honest here. But as far as a full-throated defense of my rights? Outrage over the way we were treated? Denunciation of the discriminatory culture in Roseville? Not so much.

I understood why Shad and other officers were tight-lipped in depositions. I used to be one of them. In a police department, loyalty is valued above all else. When asked to speak about the actions of another officer, we all quickly learned that less is more. We say as little as possible to protect the people we work with and for. There were repercussions for speaking up, as I found: the department might "find" a reason to discipline or even terminate an officer when the real offense was that they "weren't loyal" to people in the department.

I expected Shad to stand by me in his deposition; he told me he would. But as my lawyer peppered him with questions to get him to speak out on the discrimination he'd seen, Shad kept backing down. Shad and I had traded emails about different behaviors we'd seen in the department, and in one example, Shad wrote that Sergeant Slate was always after me to box, which I felt was discriminatory because I was a woman. But when my lawyer asked Shad about that, he became protective of Slate.

> Lawyer: You wrote in your email to Janelle, "Slate tried to make you box with us." What does that refer to?

> Begley: Sergeant Slate, he just wants everybody to come in and box, like that's his thing. I don't know why, because he's no good at it, but he encourages everyone to come in and box before work. You know, he wants people to know what it's like to be in a fight, you know, stuff like that.

> Lawyer: How about this last thing you wrote about Slate—he has documented history of sexual discrimination? What does that refer to?

> Begley: Like I said earlier, I don't have knowledge of a lot of stuff, but you hear stuff. I just heard he's discriminated against females before.

In his December 3 email to me, Shad also wrote about how Bergstrom lied to us and told us his investigation into our relationship was no big deal. He describes how Bergstrom turned off his recorder when he was interviewing Shad.

This is a pretty damning accusation, but when we asked Shad about it on the record, he backtracked.

> Lawyer: When you say [Bergstrom] lied during the investigation, what are you referencing?
>
> Begley: I don't know. Nothing comes to mind for what he lied about. I remember getting into an argument about him lying to me, and now I can't even remember what he lied about.
>
> Lawyer: You did have a pretty heated argument with him at some point, right?
>
> Begley: I did.
>
> Lawyer: Why did you have a heated argument with Lieutenant Bergstrom? What prompted that?
>
> Begley: I didn't agree with—I didn't feel like the questions that were asked during the investigation had anything to do with the sustained findings. So yeah, I guess I just thought he didn't—it was a bad investigation and it was shoddy work. And apparently, he lied to me about something, and I just can't remember what it was.

As someone who had vowed to stand by me, Shad was proving to be a weak witness for us. But after a while, we started to pry some helpful comments out of him.

Lawyer: Going back to your email to Janelle, you wrote, 'You were wrongfully terminated. I would testify to that anytime, anywhere.' Why did you believe that?

Begley: She was terminated because she was in a relationship with me, and I think she got reprimanded for being in that relationship with me. When she stuck up for herself, they fired her. To me, that's not a reason to fire somebody.

MY OWN TESTIMONY

My deposition was probably the longest of any of them. I didn't go in with any prepared speeches, but I knew that I would try to make a few points: that my termination was due to my relationship with Shad and that I'd been discriminated against on the basis of my gender and marital status.

I gave my deposition on September 3, 2014, just about two years after I'd been terminated. In the deposition, they asked me about everything—from how I was kept in training longer than the men, how Sergeant Morris insisted I read the book on emotional survival, to instances where the male supervisors in the department treated me differently than the male officers. Their attorney repeatedly asked me why I felt I'd been a victim of gender discrimination, and I made it clear: Shad had been involved in the exact same IA as I had, yet I had lost my job, and he had not. Simple as that. If what I had done had been so wrong, why had Shad not suffered the same repercussions?

Early on, we talked about the shift trade, and I recalled how I'd reviewed the past calendars in the department. I'd seen a note that someone had worked for Shad but there was never a notation that Shad had worked for his counterpart in return. I'd reviewed two months' worth of calendars, and the calendars I saw led me to believe shift trades were not consistently handled.

They asked me about Sergeant Newton. Did I think he was targeting me because of my gender?

Not before or during our conversations. But then I'd discovered the memo he'd written for Glynn, where he'd mischaracterized my attitude. I found this memo improperly placed in my file without my knowledge. At that point, my attitude about Newton changed.

> Lawyer: Did you have any concerns about Sergeant Newton such that you thought maybe he was targeting you because of your gender?
>
> Me: [...] Can I attribute that to my gender? I don't know. You know, I don't know why he made some of the comments that he did.

Lawyer: Talk about the first conversation...describe it for me.

Me: [...] I was extremely ill. I did not yell. I did not raise my voice. I was not rude. I know that for a fact. I respect supervisors and their roles. And I was very sick, and there's no way I would have crossed any line by raising my voice or yelling or being inappropriate on the phone.

Lawyer: So if Sergeant Newton were to testify that you were angry or agitated, would he be wrong?

Me: [...] If he's forming an opinion that I'm agitated because I'm asking questions about policies and procedures, then he's out of line [...]. I'm entitled to ask questions.

Lawyer: Do you have any concerns based on your interactions with Lieutenant Glynn [...]?

Me: [...] Yeah, I do have an issue with it, because I think whoever was in charge of making that decision [about that shift trade], it was gender-based because from what I've heard and what I saw in my calendar, two male officers doing a shift trade, there was no issue.

Then we moved on to the IA investigation. I described how Bergstrom had assured both Shad and me that our off-duty relationship was not part of the investigation, and that he would only look at our on-duty performance. They asked why I had concerns about the way it was conducted, and I explained that the investigation was based on cell phone records Eleanor Mann had obtained without Shad's permission. What's more, the investigator—Lieutenant Bergstrom—had assured both Shad and me that our off-duty relationship was not part of the investigation. He was only going to look at our on-duty behavior.

But when the written reprimand came out, our relationship was center stage. Walstad called it "unprofessional" and commented that we were both married with small children. Captain Moore said our behavior would not be tolerated. Their judgments were based on their moral beliefs, not on our work performance. Our relationship and our marriages were none of the department's business, I said. If we were to be penalized for having a relationship while we're both married to other people, we should have been given a chance to explain that we were both separated and going through divorces.

The department's attorney asked if anyone in a supervisory role had ever ordered Shad and me to stop seeing each other. I guess they were trying to show that there wasn't any objection to our relationship. I agreed that no one had told us to stop seeing each other, but I pointed out how our written reprimands stated that our behavior "would not be tolerated." How else was I supposed to have interpreted a statement like that? I took it to mean that they wanted Shad and me to stop seeing each other. And my interpretation was only enforced by the high-level scrutiny we were under, such as when we tried to do a simple shift trade.

Then the city's attorney asked me about Moore. She asked me about his role in the IA investigation and in the decision to terminate my probation. I said I was certain that Moore played a big role: he received the recommendation from Walstad and supported the decision to sustain the charges of conduct unbecoming and unsatisfactory work performance. I admitted that Hahn was the "ultimate decision-maker," but I also pointed out that Hahn was new to the department and that the sense around the station was that Moore was making most of the key decisions.

Moore had said as much in his own deposition.

> Lawyer: Were you involved in the decision-making process to terminate Janelle Perez?
>
> Moore: I believe so.

Moore, I believed, was inconsistent and unfair. Although Bergstrom told us he was just examining our work performance, in my mind, Moore was clearly concerned about my private relationship with Shad. He thought it was immoral and reflected badly on the department. This, as much as anything, is why I refused to sign the written reprimand.

In my view, they misrepresented the nature of the investigation, and then they drew moral conclusions about our relationship and decided to punish us for it. In my deposition, I talked about why I did not sign the written reprimand.

> Me: I didn't sign the written reprimand because I didn't agree with it. Do I think that that didn't upset him [Captain Moore] as a woman going into his office and not signing it and standing up for myself, and now to sit here and say he didn't have a hand in it? I do believe that.
>
> Roseville Lawyer: Do you have a concern that Captain Moore has a discriminatory bias against you because of your gender?
>
> Me: I do, yes.
>
> Roseville Lawyer: What is that based on?
>
> Me: [...] I think what happened in the written reprimand, his moral judgment saying we were involved in something which was not—not on duty, our relationship, and telling us in the words, you know, that we were wrong because it was a married coworker, that he was passing moral judgment [...] that it is not right for a woman at our police department to do that and I think that is what got me fired.
>
> Roseville Lawyer: [...] But I'm having a hard time connecting the dots as to what that's got to do with gender, in your mind.

Me: Well, the bottom line is I was terminated because of my relationship with Shad Begley. I'm a woman. He's a man. He still has his position at the police department [...]. My belief is that Captain Moore had a hand in it. I'm sure it upset him that I stood up for myself as a woman and refused to sign the written reprimand. But I did. I did not believe that I violated those two policy sections. So I suffered, and Shad Begley did not. And he's still employed there. I cannot see how that's not gender discrimination.

I felt like I was under attack from the city's lawyers through the entire deposition. I felt like I was having to prove myself the entire time. But I also knew I had to stick to my guns. I knew the department could hide behind the fact that while I was on probation, they could get rid of me without providing a reason. But that doesn't mean they could fire me for any reason at all. In fact, the department ended up giving a reason for firing me, and their reasoning seemed discriminatory to me. That's what I couldn't—and still can't—accept. Roseville employed some officers who allegedly traded wives and had recreational sex with strangers. It employed male officers who flaunted the tobacco policy. Male officers routinely ignored rules and procedures, like the shift trades. But when a woman comes along and stands up for herself and doesn't roll over, she's labeled a problem. Let's get rid of her.

I also had to keep coming back to my performance. There

was not one shred of evidence that my work performance during probation was anything but exemplary. I was an experienced, proactive officer who helped out her team and actually *looked* for work to do while other officers watched the clock and left immediately at the end of their shift. During a field training officer's meeting shortly after I was fired, I heard one of the field training officers had asked Lieutenant Richardson if I was fired for something related to work performance, and Richardson said my termination had nothing to do with performance. My last supervisor, Sergeant Stanton, sent me an email telling me I was a good cop.

I *was* a good cop.

At one point, their lawyer asked me what career opportunities I had looked into since leaving the police department. I was offended by the question. I told the lawyer my job now was to get my old job back. That's what I was dedicated to.

> Me: So I'm not going to rush into starting a business or going to school [...]. This is what I'm passionate about. I was an excellent police officer, I enjoyed the career, and I want to go back to it.
>
> Lawyer: When you say "This is what I'm passionate about," do you mean law enforcement?

Me: About standing up for my rights as a woman and taking on this case.

I admitted to suffering from depression and anxiety. That's a taboo subject for most police officers, but I acknowledged that this had been a very hard time in my life. I'd lost my job, my career. And everyone else involved still had their jobs in their lives. I was the one who lost everything.

The lawyer also wanted proof that my professional reputation had been damaged as a result of my termination. Well, stories about me had been in the news media, and I knew people were forming judgments about my character—the way Moore and Walstad had. How could that *not* affect my reputation? No one was hearing the full story. The administrators in Roseville didn't hear the whole story, and they concluded that I was a problem. I expected the same thing would happen in other police departments.

When my lawyer and I filed the lawsuit in US District Court, we didn't ask for a specific dollar amount, but I wanted my job and seniority restored. I wanted an apology. I also asked for back pay, compensation for emotional pain, punitive damages, and attorney's fees.

Our complaint ran twenty pages, and we had testimony that backed up every point we'd made in our case.

In the end, none of this made any difference to the district court.

SUMMARY JUDGMENT

In the spring of 2015, Roseville filed a motion for summary judgment, and the district court in Sacramento set a date for oral arguments. Essentially, a motion for summary judgment is when a party to a lawsuit asks the court to decide a claim without a trial. If the motion is denied, you go to trial. If the motion is granted, the case is over.

On my way to court, I got stuck in traffic and was running later than I wanted to be. I entered the courtroom just as the hearing was about to start.

My lawyers, Sean O'Dowd and Paul Goyette, were both there, and during his presentation, it appeared to me that O'Dowd got pounded. I don't know if this was the first case he'd ever argued in a courtroom, but it didn't go well at all. It was hard for me to watch. I felt he needed to be much more aggressive in his presentation, and walking out of the court, I felt terrible. I thought, *I deserve to lose after how poorly we presented our case.*

We waited a long time for the court's ruling on Roseville's motion for summary judgment. I was checking online every day to see if a decision had been filed. On June 11, 2015,

O'Dowd wrote to say he expected a ruling soon and was surprised at how long it was taking. In the meantime, he said, we should consider mediating the case in August.

O'Dowd reminded me that we didn't have to settle at mediation if the offer wasn't right. He told me it would be a mistake to not at least hear an offer from the city to gauge what they were willing to do to rectify my experience. Still, I didn't want to budge. I wasn't interested in settling the case with money—I still wanted my job back, and I wanted justice.

On June 19, the district court granted Roseville's motion for summary judgment. I found the decision online before Goyette notified me or could explain what the decision meant. I was angry that Goyette hadn't gotten in touch with me, angry because I felt my case had been presented so weakly by O'Dowd, and anxious about what the decision on the screen really meant. I emailed Goyette. "Are we awaiting anything else," I asked, "or did I essentially lose this whole thing?"

The district court concluded that Hahn, Moore, Walstad, and the police department deserved "qualified immunity" because I did not have a clearly established constitutional right to engage in a personal relationship with Shad while on duty. The court also claimed there was no evidence that stigmatizing information about me was published in connection with my termination. Finally, the court ruled that I did not provide sufficient evidence that Hahn's reasons for firing me were a pretext for sex discrimination or that my gender was a motivating factor in the decision-making process.

I was devastated. In tears. I couldn't let it end like this.

Still, I was running out of options. My career in law enforcement seemed like it was over.

I met with Goyette and laid it all out for him. "I'm not ready to quit," I said. "What are my options?"

Goyette agreed to appeal the district court's summary judgment.

We decided to appeal the summary judgment to the Ninth Circuit Court of Appeals in San Francisco. Goyette said he knew an attorney, Richard Paul Fisher, who specialized in these appeals and knew the Ninth Circuit Court very well.

One more time, I held on to hope.

CHAPTER 7

THE APPEAL

In July 2015, I signed the paperwork to appeal the district court's summary judgment. It would be nearly two years before my case would be heard in court.

In late April 2016, still awaiting the hearing, I had one mediation session with the city of Roseville. I thought it would be a waste of time, but the attorneys said it was part of the process, so I hired a babysitter and took the time to attend the session.

Hahn was there. Just seeing him made me feel sick. The attorneys and other people in the room were all joking and laughing like old friends, but it was difficult for me. I could not fake it and pretend that I was happy to see any of these people.

The mediator put us in separate rooms and began the process of going back and forth for the negotiations. I wanted compensation for the considerable investment I'd made pursuing the lawsuit. The city's first offer was so low, I was appalled. They offered around $6,000.

"Are you kidding me?" I asked. I told the mediator that I would take nothing less than full payment for all of my attorneys' fees. "If that's something they're not willing to do, then there's no reason to be here," I said. After all these years, a big part of me was just ready for this all to be over. For me to be able to stop replaying different situations that happened, over and over in my head. I knew in my heart and will always believe that I was terminated because of discriminatory reasons.

"I don't think they'll go for that," the mediator said but then left the room to talk to the other party.

"You know," Goyette said to me. "Something is always better than nothing."

I wasn't going to hear it.

"*I did all this work and went through all of this emotional distress, and you want me to take some small handout so I'll just go away?*" I thought. "*I'm not doing that.*"

The mediator came back. Roseville was not interested in my offer.

"Okay," I said. "Then we're done." I gathered up my things and walked out.

THE PIVOTAL QUESTION

In the words of one of the Ninth Circuit Court judges, my case focused on the question of "How much control the government can force individuals to cede over their private lives in exchange for the privilege of serving the public by means of government employment." Did public employees like me have a right to privacy in our personal lives?

In addressing this question, the court warned that "as a society" we can't allow government to use its authority as an employer to encroach on our private lives, or even, as Ninth Circuit Judge Stephen Reinhardt put it, "eliminate the development of ordinary human emotions from the workplace."

"We have long recognized that officers and employees of a police department enjoy a right of privacy in 'private, off-duty' sexual behavior," Reinhardt wrote.

Stephen Reinhardt was known as the "liberal lion" of the Ninth Circuit Court. He'd been appointed by President Jimmy Carter and had been a supporter of several liberal causes, including same-sex marriage, abortion, and doctor-aided suicide. He was in his late eighties but remained active on the court. His conservative critics, like William Rehnquist of the Supreme Court, said the Ninth Circuit under Reinhardt had a reputation for having "a hard time saying 'no' to any litigant with a hard-luck story."

Another way to think of that criticism: Reinhardt was a judge who actually listened to all sides of a story. That sounded good to me.

ORAL ARGUMENTS

Paul Goyette had Richard Paul Fisher argue my case before the Ninth Circuit. The hearing was held on April 19, 2017. Three justices heard the arguments—Reinhardt, A. Wallace Tashima, and Donald W. Molloy. Although I couldn't attend the hearing, Fisher sent me a video of it, and I probably watched the proceedings about fifty times that night.

Fisher, a trim man with graying hair, did an excellent job. He cut right to heart of the issue: the reasons Hahn gave for terminating me—that I didn't get along with women in the department, the citizen complaint that had never been investigated, and my supposedly angry call with Sergeant Newton—were "not worthy of credence." The district court, he said, is required to look at the evidence in the fairest possible light to me, but it had not done that and had granted Roseville the summary judgment instead.

The district court, Fisher argued, had disregarded an emotional and crucial aspect of the case: "the age-old problem of men judging the sexual behavior of women."

"That's the elephant in the room in this case," he said.

Fisher described how the department, realizing they couldn't use my off-duty behavior as a reason to terminate me, had "reversed course" and dreamed up other reasons to let me go.

"The reason they made the reversal was they allowed the male to escape unscathed," Fisher said. "Only the woman [...] lost her employment."

Fisher quickly discredited the city's stated reasons for firing me. The claim that I didn't get along with female officers wasn't true because there were only six females, and I hadn't worked directly with any of them. The citizen's complaint was a "thin reed" because the complainant had never formally filed a complaint, and her accusations were never investigated. The call with Newton was mischaracterized by Hahn because I hadn't raised my voice or shown Newton any disrespect during the call. Clearly, Fisher argued, these accusations were an attempt to camouflage the fact that Hahn had illegally terminated me for moral reasons based on my relationship with Shad.

"The record, I believe, is shot through with pieces of evidence that suggest the motivation here was improper and did focus on what the department viewed as sexual transgression of a woman but nonetheless taking action that let the man off scot-free," Fisher said.

Watching the hearing, I was struck by how knowledgeable Reinhardt was about my case. He had clearly read the depositions we had taken.

When Roseville's attorney, Stacey Sheston, began her arguments, Reinhardt immediately made it clear that he felt the matter needed to go to trial.

"The question is what was the motivation [of the chief]?" Reinhardt said. "Did sexual conduct play a part in their decision to terminate her? Sexual conduct is protected by the Constitution."

When Sheston tried to argue that my affair with Shad did not factor into Hahn's decision to terminate me, Reinhardt would have none of it. Why was Janelle Perez released from probation? It wasn't because of the cell phone conversations. It wasn't because of a citizen's complaint or trouble getting along with female officers. It wasn't the phone call with Newton. "Well, that's what they came up with when they corrected their decision after she was discharged," Reinhardt concluded.

Reinhardt pulled out Hahn's deposition and read the part where the chief admitted the IA investigation into my relationship with Shad was one of the "red flags" that led to my termination. Reinhardt read sections where the chief admitted that our cell phone calls were insignificant. What stands out, Reinhardt said, was the pervasive moral judgments made by supervisors in the department during and after Bergstrom's IA investigation. This suggests their true motivation for firing me was their moral beliefs, he said, and firing me for those reasons is unconstitutional.

"If you can take those inferences into account, then you have a question of motivation," the judge explained. "Motivation is generally a question of fact to be decided by a jury."

In the Ninth Circuit decision that followed, Reinhardt wrote:

> Given the investigation of charges based upon allegations related to her affair with another officer, the evidence of the investigators' moral disapproval of her affair, and the Department's constantly shifting justifications for her termination, as well as the independent reasons for doubting the legitimacy of each shifting justification, we conclude that a genuine issue of material fact exists as to whether Perez was fired at least in part because of her extramarital affair.

THE APPEAL IS GRANTED

The court's decision was released in February 2018. Reinhardt, Molloy, and Tashima reversed the summary judgment on my claim that my rights to privacy and intimate association were violated. That part of my case could go to trial. However, the judges affirmed summary judgment on my claims regarding due process and gender discrimination, which meant we wouldn't be taking those issues before a jury. Our case was remanded back to the district court.

This was a significant victory, and I was overjoyed to read Reinhardt's analysis of the case. I felt like he was the first person in the legal system who had actually taken the time to read through my case and understand what happened to me.

"As a society, we must remain solicitous of the constitutional liberties of public employees, as of any citizens, to the greatest degree possible, and should be careful not to allow the State to use its authority as an employer to encroach excessively or unnecessarily upon the areas of private life, such as family relationships, procreation, and sexual conduct, where an individual's dignitary interest in autonomy is at its apex," Reinhardt wrote. "Nor can or should we seek to eliminate the development of ordinary human emotions from the workplace where we spend a good part of our waking hours."

The other justices concurred with Reinhardt, but one of them—Tashima—did not agree with the reasons behind the decision. Tashima wrote a short opinion noting that I was a probationary officer who could be fired at will for no cause. However, after litigation began, Tashima said the department gave three reasons for firing me. Those three reasons, Tashima said, "arose in such short order after the internal affairs review that a reasonable inference may be drawn that they may have been pretextual," meaning that they were camouflage for their real reasons for firing me.

At this point, I felt 100 percent certain that if I could get my case in front of a jury that I would win. How could I *not* win? The judges who had taken the time to sort through everything could see what Roseville had done. An employer should not decide who you can have a relationship with off duty.

The Ninth Circuit Court of Appeals decision read:

> Any reasonable official would have been on notice that, viewing the facts in the light most favorable to her, Perez's termination was unconstitutional.
>
> In other words, under our precedent, the Constitution is violated when a public employee is terminated at least in part on the basis of protected conduct, such as her private, off-duty sexual activity. We conclude that Perez has provided sufficient evidence of each element to survive summary judgment.

The appeal court was particularly critical of Hahn, saying his "testimony is inconsistent."

Hahn had stated that my private, off-duty relationship with Shad "was not a factor in the decision to release her from probation." But in his deposition, Hahn was asked if the IA investigation into my relationship with Shad influenced his decision to fire me, and he responded by saying, "I would say it was part of it."

Reinhardt wasn't fooled by this seeming double-talk.

"A reasonable factfinder could conclude on the basis of Hahn's testimony alone that Perez's termination was motivated in part by the revelation of her extramarital affair with Begley," the judge concluded.

Hahn wasn't alone. The court pointed out that Captain Moore was also motivated "in part" to fire me because of my affair with Shad. Even though he wasn't the decision-maker in my case, Moore nevertheless had a great deal of influence, and he had admitted that the affair was "significant" to him because it "presented a truly ethical dilemma whether or not that is something that could reflect unfavorably on the police department."

Walstad's behavior didn't go unnoticed either. Walstad was clear that he felt my relationship with Shad was unprofessional and improper, and that further supported the court's conclusion that the department "morally disapproved" of my private sexual conduct and terminated me in part because of that conduct.

Hahn's contention was that my termination was based on the three, last-minute discoveries—that I didn't get along with the female officers, that I'd angered a domestic violence complainant, and that I'd had a "bad attitude" during my call with Newton regarding the shift change. But the judges concluded it was unclear whether these were the real reasons for my termination.

Again, from the Ninth Circuit decision:

> Based on the evidence that Walstad and Moore morally disapproved of Perez's sexual conduct, and the speed with which these unrelated employment issues were "discovered" immediately after the IA investigation revealed Perez's affair, a reasonable factfinder could conclude that all three reasons were pretexts for an impermissible motive.

As I read the decision, I finally felt validated. After years of Hahn, Walstad, and Moore denying what they'd done, the court had finally seen the truth.

"I told you so," my dad said when I shared the decision with him. "You just needed the right people to hear you."

IMPERMISSIBLE MOTIVES

We didn't get everything we wanted, however.

Reinhardt upheld the summary judgment ruling that my due process rights had not been violated. We'd argued that the department had violated my rights when Moore mailed his letter to Eleanor, telling her that two charges against me had been sustained. To me, that was "stigmatizing information" that had been published about me. As a result, I felt I had a due process right to give my side of the story. The Ninth Circuit found that the district court had made a mistake when it concluded that the letter was not "published," but they also concluded that Hahn, Moore, and Walstad were entitled to "qualified immunity."

Reinhardt also said the summary judgment denying my claim of sex discrimination was affirmed because it was the extramarital affair and not gender discrimination that prompted my termination.

Still, the court decided that the district court's grant of summary judgment in favor of the city of Roseville should be reversed on my right to privacy claim.

The court explained that a police department can violate its employees' rights to privacy and intimate association either by "impermissibly investigating their private sexual conduct or by taking adverse employment action on the basis of such private conduct."

But the court did say that it was unconstitutional to fire me for having an affair unless the department could show that my on-the-job performance suffered.

The department never did that. All three judges affirmed: I deserved a trial. I deserved to be heard.

CHAPTER 8

THE DEATH OF A JUDGE

After the decision was published, my lawyers and I weren't sure what would happen next. The city of Roseville could file a petition for an appeal to the US Supreme Court. But a month after the ruling came out, we learned that one of the judges in the Ninth Circuit had requested an en banc review, in which the Ninth Circuit would have an entire slate of judges—not just the three-judge panel—review the case. Goyette told me that in significant cases like mine, it was common for the court to review its own decision. "We are waiting for that to run its course," Goyette wrote in his email, "and then we will probably be back on the trial track." He thought it might be about a month before we'd hear whether the en banc review was granted.

While we waited for news of the en banc hearing, my dad called me out of the blue on March 29. "Don't freak out," he began.

I took a breath.

"It's Judge Reinhardt, who heard your case. He died today."

I felt sad at the news Reinhardt had passed away. He had championed my case and been an advocate for me. But I didn't imagine his death would affect the ruling; the decision was already published. My dad agreed there seemed to be nothing to worry about. The judges' opinion had been published a month before Reinhardt's death. We sat tight and waited to hear the outcome of the en banc review.

For some reason that neither I nor my lawyer could discern, the court wouldn't make a decision on whether the new hearing would take place or not. Months ticked by. Then a year. My case sat, unable to go to court.

REVERSAL OF FATE

In May of 2019, over a year after Reinhardt's death, I got an email from my lawyer out of the blue. My case had been reheard. My lawyer hadn't been notified the case was being reviewed. Somehow, we'd lost.

The Ninth Circuit decision had been reversed, just like that. I was stunned.

The new decision had nothing to do with the en banc

request, which was still pending. I never learned who had decided my case should be reheard or how it could be reheard so swiftly.

My lawyer later learned that the Ninth Circuit was reviewing many of the decisions Reinhardt made just prior to his death. A new panel of judges had reviewed our case. Tashima was back and so was Molloy, but Reinhardt was replaced by Judge Sandra Ikuta. They issued a new opinion.

The panel affirmed the district court's summary judgment in favor of Roseville.

We'd won, and then we'd lost. And I couldn't, and still can't, wrap my head around it. The injustice! Here we go again, this time a US appeals court making up their own rules. I couldn't find any documentation stating this was legal—the decision had been decided, published, and even used as a precedent in similar cases—therefore, it should have stood unless being reversed by an en banc hearing.

In the new Ninth Circuit opinion, Ikuta contended that none of the legal precedents had established that a police department is "constitutionally prohibited from considering an officer's off-duty sexual relationship in making a decision to terminate her, where there is specific evidence that the officer engaged in on-the-job conduct in connection with that relationship."

For the "specific evidence" that my on-the-job conduct had been affected by my relationship with Shad, Ikuta leaned on the descriptions of our cell phone use. Ikuta seemed to be obsessed with the cell phone violation, which was not cited as a reason for my termination and wasn't sustained until *after* I'd been let go.

We could have addressed this in a hearing, but we were never granted one. The entire case was reviewed with no lawyers present, no questions asked, no clarification given.

This new opinion granted "qualified immunity" to the police department and its supervisors because, the judges said, it was not clearly established that my constitutional rights had been violated. I couldn't believe it—if it wasn't "clearly established" that my constitutional rights had been violated, then shouldn't my case go to trial to make sure that question was resolved?

In Ikuta's mind, Hahn had "confirmed" that my relationship with Shad had not influenced his decision to terminate me. Although Hahn had originally disagreed with Moore's recommendation to fire me after the first written reprimand, "he understood it was best practice to 'release someone from probation rather than impose lower-level discipline where low-level misconduct had been determined to have occurred,'" Ikuta wrote.

We conclude that [legal precedents] are not so clear that every reasonable official would understand that terminating Perez because of her ongoing extramarital relationship with Begley violated her constitutional right to privacy.

Rather, in this case, an internal affairs investigation resulted in a report with specific and detailed findings that Perez used her personal cell phone to call and text Begley while on duty, including while driving her police vehicle and responding to calls for service. As a result of this personal phone usage, Perez was issued a written reprimand that tied the phone usage to her relationship with Begley and concluded that the phone usage entailed "clear policy violations" and was "inefficient, contrary to good order, and ultimately reflected negatively on the department."

As I read the decision, inside I screamed, *WRONG, WRONG, WRONG!* I was never given a reprimand for a cell phone policy violation. I thought to myself, *How can an educated judge seemingly skim over the record and deliver a decision without demonstrating a clear understanding of this case? How can she not see or address that Chief Hahn's testimony is riddled with inconsistencies?* I wondered to myself whether she knew someone at the Roseville Police Department, or Chief Hahn, or was just such a staunch supporter of police departments that despite all evidence, they could do no wrong in her eyes.

This time, the vote was split between the judges, 2-1. Ikuta voted to affirm the district court. In the last line of her opinion, Ikuta justified her decision by writing that "[Perez] conceded that the alleged discrimination was not actually based on her gender."

I had never said any such thing. In all the years I'd been fighting the lawsuit, I consistently maintained that my gender was most certainly the reason I'd faced discrimination. I couldn't believe I was seeing such a blatant falsehood in a legal document written by a judge.

Somehow, though, none of the details of the case had changed, one of the judges changed his mind between the first hearing and the second. Tashima—who had been on the original panel and voted in my favor the first time—changed colors and sided with Ikuta.

Molloy dissented and stuck by his opinion from the first hearing. The original panel had "correctly resolved this issue," he observed, and it was wrong to substitute a new judge for Reinhardt.

"Perez's appeal was decided by a quorum of the judges on the original panel, the decision was published, and there was an en banc call by a member of this court," Molloy wrote.

"Consequently, the original opinion should stand. It was

decided. Now with a different judge assigned, the new majority opinion completely reverses the original opinion without notice to the parties or regard to the en banc call. Judge Reinhardt's death [...] should not be invoked to reverse the outcome of the case legitimately decided by the original majority through a procedural mechanism of substituting a different judge."

Ironically, if the en banc review had gone through, I'm confident I would have won. The en banc hearing would have ensured my case would be heard by a full panel of judges of the Ninth Circuit Court of Appeals. Instead, my case was reviewed by just three. And one of them, Tashima, had already been poised to change his mind and tilt the scales of justice against me.

OUT OF OPTIONS

Paul Goyette asked the Ninth Circuit to conduct an en banc review of this latest decision, but our request was turned down within a month. I couldn't believe it. The previous en banc hearing request had dragged on for over a year with no decision, and yet our request was turned down almost immediately. I couldn't wrap my mind around how this process worked. Was the court system exempt from deadlines? How could there be such a long wait for the previous en banc request and such a swift strike-down of our request? If the court had made a timely decision on the first en banc review, my case would have been back in the district court for a jury trial before Reinhardt's death and the court's next move.

Next, Goyette and Richard Paul Fisher consulted a US Supreme Court expert in Washington, D.C., to determine if we should appeal to the highest court.

The news wasn't good.

Before the case had been reheard and reversed, the D.C. consultant had been interested in defending my case if the city took their appeal to the Supreme Court. The question at the center of my case—whether someone who worked a government job still had a right to privacy in her relationships and sexual conduct—was an important one, and the D.C. consultant thought our case could be strong enough to win.

But when the appeal was reversed, Ikuta's opinion was carefully written to shift the context of the case. By focusing heavily on the cell phone violation—the violation I was never found "guilty" of while I was employed by the city of Roseville—Ikuta claimed my relationship had affected my on-duty conduct, and *that's* what I'd been fired for. According to Ikuta, the phone calls I made on my breaks at work cost me my privacy. The D.C. consultant said the way the new decision was written made it next to impossible to argue at the Supreme Court level. The case, Goyette relayed to me, "would have no chance of success."

"The new decision carefully crafted the facts in such a way that the Supreme Court would not have any need to review or correct the decision," he wrote. "The new decision emphasized the 'qualified immunity' defense, which the Supreme Court favors very strongly right now."

Then Goyette hit the last nail into the coffin:

"Based on this recommendation and our team's extensive research and work on this case, we believe we can go no further and that your case has completely run its course."

Seven years after I'd been fired—after seven years of fighting—it was all over.

ONE LAST LETTER

Though I had no legal recourse left, I made one last attempt to be heard by the justice system. I wrote a letter to the chief judge of the Ninth Circuit Court of Appeals, Chief Justice Sidney Thomas. I wanted him to see the miscarriage of justice that was so apparent to me.

I sent copies of the letter to numerous women's rights groups, as well as the Ninth Circuit Court of Appeals.

I wanted to be heard, and more than that, I wanted accountability from the judges who so swiftly reheard and dismissed my case. After summing up the details—the initial decision, the en banc request that languished for over a year, the death of Reinhardt, the swift hearing in front of Ikuta—I expressed my shock at the unfairness of the process. "Can you please explain to me how this was legally appropriate?" I pleaded. After describing how my own en banc request had been so quickly dismissed, I wanted to know: "How is this a fair and legitimate process?" I continued:

> This issue that was heard on April 19, 2017 is not only an important legal matter to me personally, but also to the many women in present and future generations who may feel similarly discriminated against in their places of employment. I don't understand how the court can make such a rash decision to rehear this case. This deserves an answer and the answer is not clearly found in the latest decision dated May 21, 2019. Judge Ikuta's decision and Judge Molloy's dissent show very different stances on this. I seek clarification on this decision from you directly as the Chief Judge of the Ninth Circuit.

I explained all the other factors of the new decision that I found so difficult to understand. That Tashima had changed his opinion even though no new details had come to light in the case. That Ikuta had weighed the cell phone violation so heavily in her decision, even though Hahn had admitted the cell phone use hadn't played a role in my termination. That Ikuta mistakenly believed I'd changed my stance on the role gender played in the discrimination against me. I doubted that Ikuta had correctly read and understood the case. How, after such a miscarriage of justice, could there be no recourse?

> One of the most critical aspects in a civil case is to allow me to have my day in court and a jury of my peers to decide the fundamental aspects of the case and render a just and fair decision. All I am asking for is a fair and impartial review by the courts, so this case can be adjudicated lawfully and within the full parameters of the law.
>
> Regards,
>
> Janelle Perez

At the time of this writing, I have gotten no response from Chief Justice Thomas. Honestly, I don't expect a response. But I do believe I deserve one.

CONCLUSION

I wish my story didn't end here, but unfortunately, it does. After being fired by the city of Roseville, I never returned to law enforcement. It saddens me to think that law enforcement lost an excellent, well-rounded police officer—exactly what we need *more* of.

By contrast, Asher Martin was promoted at the time of this writing. What I observed as his rude and inappropriate behavior and his own IA investigation while on probation apparently left no black marks on his record.

Newton was made a lieutenant. Bergstrom and Glynn each made captain. After many years of hard work, Brzyscz finally made sergeant and is still at Roseville PD. Shad is now at a police department in West Sacramento, and Mary Green is an investigator with the district attorney's office. Moore, Walstad, and Morris have all retired from Roseville.[4]

And as of this writing in 2020, out of over 120 police officers in Roseville, less than ten of them are female. I'm sad to see that not much has changed in regard to gender diversity since I worked there in 2012.

Lastly, Hahn is now the chief of the Sacramento Police Department, a position he took in 2017. An article in *The Sacramento Bee* looked back at Hahn's time at Roseville:

> Hahn encountered a department used to running the way it had always run, a place where people sometimes worked covertly to undermine him, said Ray Kerridge, the former Roseville city manager who held the same job in Sacramento.
>
> "Daniel wanted to be Mr. Nice Guy, and when you've been in this business long enough, you realize that is a luxury you can't afford," Kerridge said. [...] Hahn said he put up with some people on his team who were not 100 percent committed to improving the department, a mistake he said he won't make again.[5]

---

4   According to the Roseville Police Department Facebook page, the Roseville Police Department website (roseville.ca.us), and transparentcalifornia.com.

5   Marcos Bretón, "New Police Chief Breaks the Mold—Not Just Because He Is Black," *The Sacramento Bee*, July 3, 2017.

Reading this article, I cringed. Though the journalist hadn't named the people who "worked covertly to undermine" Hahn, my mind leaped to people like Captain Moore. Hahn had gone along with Moore's decision-making in my case. He was a newer chief at the time, and he didn't push back against Walstad and Moore. Despite Hahn's commitment to improving the department, in my case, he never admitted to the mistakes I believe he made. Throughout my termination and the lawsuit and depositions that followed, Hahn refused to take responsibility for his decisions in my case.

Around the same time, Hahn was interviewed in *Western City* on his vision for community policing. He described the ideal characteristics of police officers by saying, "Ninety-nine percent of our job is relating to people [...]. If you are one of those people who can come into a situation and calm everybody down with your voice, that is what we want."[6]

That's the kind of police officer I was. Where I saw many of my male colleagues resort to physical methods first and rush to restrain someone, I used my voice. My police work aligned with what was needed in the community, yet I was fired over moralistic judgments about what I was doing in my off-duty time.

---

6 Charles Harvey and Eva Spiegel, "Community Policing Insights from Chief Daniel Hahn," *Western City*, September 25, 2018.

In the same article, Hahn described how many people across the country don't have trusting relationships with law enforcement. "People have to know the department is willing to look at itself and make changes," he concluded. But I had not seen Hahn or the department's supervisors being willing to look honestly at their actions or take responsibility. I felt they used their power not to change the department for the better but to cover their own tracks and protect their careers, at the expense of mine.

I still feel angry. I don't know when I'm going to get over it. I don't think about what happened every day like I used to, but when I do think about it, I can feel the anger rising up inside me.

It comforts me to think about karma, and how karma is going to come back on those who destroyed my career. I imagine that someday, one of the male supervisors who judged me will have a daughter or a spouse who is discriminated against, and the experience is going to slap them in the face. I believe there are always consequences to your actions. Look at my consequences: I got involved in a relationship with Shad, and I lost my career. There aren't many consequences more serious than that.

But my anger keeps me fired up to speak my story and stand up against the discrimination I faced. Today, I'm raising my children to be advocates for those who are being bullied. I teach my sons to stand up to kids who are being picked on at school, even if they're not friends. I'm fiercely protective of my daughter. I'm afraid of the mistakes she might make. I worry she'll disregard my advice, as I disregarded my dad's. And even as I worry for her, I recognize it's not her decisions I'm afraid of—it's how I fear the world will treat her.

The environment we live in is riddled with inequality. The fact that discriminatory behavior continues to occur in the workplace with no consequence for inappropriate actions goes to show how far we still have to go to overcome the disgust of misogyny. My daughter is growing up in a world that still discriminates against women just as harshly as I was discriminated against. I want to change that world for my daughter, just as I want to change that world for you.

I've learned through this experience that standing strong in one's story is hard. So often in the years of my court case, I questioned myself. All my effort, my time, my energy, and my anger—was it worth it? Was I crazy to keep standing up for myself? Should I just let the case go, just roll over and settle, just let myself be walked over? Each time I heard the facts of my story twisted by Walstad or Moore or Hahn, self-doubt seeped into me.

In all this time, I needed to be supported, and I needed to be believed. More than getting my job back or recovering all the money I'd spent on attorneys' fees, what my day in court represented was a chance to be heard, and for someone in power to say, *yes, this really happened.*

In the absence of someone in power standing up for me, I had to stand up for myself. The more I stood up, the more resolved I became. I got stronger, fiercer, more passionate, more certain. I made the mistake of not taking my story to the media and the public at the beginning of my case. I wish I had exposed the injustice earlier instead of respecting a legal process that never respected me. I was shooed away, pushed aside, and silenced, and each time I was beaten down, I relived my pain all over again. I also found my courage all over again, each and every time.

It takes a multitude of us to stand up and speak out against the injustice we face. While I don't wish my experience of injustice on anyone, I want to hear from those who have stories like mine. I'm inspired by all the women I've seen stand up for themselves in their lifetimes and pave the way for others who come behind them. With every story I hear, I'm given a push toward my courage. I share mine because I believe it will give others the push they need.

If you have experienced injustice, I hope you'll share your story with me. I will listen to you and support you. We are all different, and we are all entitled to live our lives the way we want to outside the workplace. Our private lives are up to us, not the people in power.

I know that when I share my story, and you share yours, we can inspire others to stand up. If our individual voices are too faint to be heard, our collective voices will be a roar.

And someday soon, the people in power—superiors at work, judges in courts, men who get preferential treatment over women—will finally listen.

ACKNOWLEDGMENTS

Above all, I thank you, Dad. Throughout it all, you've been my number one supporter. When reflecting back on the past eight years of my life, you've been the only person who has stayed true to me. When others judged me and turned their backs on me, you stood by me and supported me in my weakest moments. Without your love, support, and encouragement, I may have never had the courage to fight the fight I did. Thank you, Dad, for loving me despite all of my imperfections.

Thank you, Jason—you are the most selfless human I have ever met. For you to support me in this crazy endeavor shows how amazing a man you are.

Thank you to all the people who know how to say, "I am sorry," and mean it. We are all imperfect humans, and once we can admit when we are wrong or faltering, we have learned a truly important life lesson.

I'm incredibly grateful for the women who have come before me and given a voice to the discrimination they have suffered. To those who stood up to the bigotry and fought against the bullies, your strength and courage are what allowed me to find mine.

For those who have discriminated against me, thank you for waking me up to show me how much further we need to go in our fight for equality. You've awoken the person inside me who will fight against injustice done toward others.

ABOUT THE AUTHOR

JANELLE PEREZ graduated from The Pennsylvania State University with a degree in administration of justice and sociology. She was a police officer in the Bay Area for six years before accepting a position with the Roseville Police Department. After only eight months, Janelle was unfairly terminated and began a seven-year fight for her career, livelihood, and reputation in the court system. An advocate for female leadership in law enforcement, Janelle strongly believes in the value of the female perspective in the field.